Supporting Emotional Needs of the Gifted

30 Essays on Giftedness
30 Years of SENG

Edited by SENG

SENG is a 501(c)(3) non-profit organization
SENG
P.O. Box 488
Poughquag, NY 12570
http://www.sengifted.org
office@sengifted.org
(845)797-5054

Contents

With Gratitude to the Contributors to this Collection

Angela Arenivar
Rose Blackett
Dina Brulles
Marc Caplan
Lori Comallie-Caplan
Christine Fonseca
Rosina M. Gallagher
Jean Goerss
Judith Wynn Halsted
Jane Hesslein
Holly Hughes
Joseph Hughes
Tiombe-Bisa Kendrick
Carolyn Kottmeyer
Marianne Kuzujanakis
Sharon Lind
Linda Neumann
Vidisha Patel
Steven Pfeiffer
Sheri Plybon
Michael Postma
Amy Price
Helen Prince
Carol Raymond
Sylvia Rimm
Lisa Rivero
Beverly Shaklee
Michael Shaughnessy
Wenda Sheard
Jeremy Tardy
James T. Webb

Introduction

T hank you for your purchase of this collection of thirty of the most popular articles and essays from SENG's online library. Thirty years ago, SENG (Supporting Emotional Needs of the Gifted) was formed to bring attention to the unique emotional needs of gifted children and to provide adults with guidance, information, resources, and a forum to communicate about raising and educating these children. While many schools, communities, and organizations focus on the *intellectual* potential of gifted individuals, SENG brings attention to the unique *social and emotional needs* of all gifted individuals, needs which are often misunderstood or ignored.

Today, SENG has expanded its reach and focus to include not only gifted children, but also gifted adults. SENG programs include our flagship SENG Model Parent Groups (SMPGs), in which parents of gifted children learn to help each other to understand and discuss their children's social and emotional needs, continuing education classes and credits for mental health professionals and educators, SENGinars (SENG webinars) presented by experts in giftedness and gifted education, an extensive free online library database, the *SENGVine* monthly newsletter of announcements and resources, an annual conference, and much more.

SENG is an independent, non-profit 501(c)(3) organization

with a diverse Board of Directors. If the articles in this book touch you or help you in any way, please consider making a tax-deductible donation to help us to continue to support the needs of gifted individuals and to offer even more programs and services. Learn more and donate online at http://www.sengifted.org.

About the Essays

The thirty essays and articles in the pages that follow were all written for and previously published by SENG, many by current and former SENG Directors. They are grouped thematically.

Part One, "The SENG Difference," features articles about SENG's history, programs, and impact, beginning with Jane Hesslein's perspective on "Coming Full-Circle" from finding SENG at its beginning to now being on its Board of Directors. SENG Founder James T. Webb shares some of SENG's history. Carol Raymond writes about what she has learned from being a SENG Model Parent Group facilitator, and SENG's first Executive Director, Amy Price, tells a personal account of how SENG changed her life and her family.

Part Two, "Understanding Giftedness," provides information about what giftedness feels and looks like. SENG's first President, Sharon Lind, explains the concept of overexcitability as it relates to giftedness, followed by an article by Jean Goerss on asynchronous development. Former Board Member Beverly Shaklee describes giftedness in young children, and Patricia Schuler tackles the important topic of teasing and gifted children. SENG Editor-in-Chief Michael Shaughnessy interviews Sylvia Rimm on perfectionism in the gifted. This section ends with SENG Director Rose Blackett's discussion of recognizing and assessing creativity.

Part Three, "Not Just for Parents," is a selection of essays that offer advice for parents, teachers, and others who care about supporting the social and emotional needs of gifted children and adolescents. This section begins with strategies from Christine Fonseca to help kids (and parents) cope with typical behavior issues. Judith Wynn Halsted offers tips for using books to meet the social and emotional needs of gifted children. Former SENG Director Steven Pfeiffer writes about how to encourage emotional intelligence, and Dina Brulles, also a former SENG Director, discusses parenting children who are twice-exceptional. Former SENG President Wenda Sheard offers back-to-school suggestions for how parents can support their children, and SENG Director Carolyn Kottmeyer reflects on what she wishes she had known sooner about gifted education. Former SENG Director Linda Neumann writes about the differences between how we treat the intellectually and athletically gifted. In a two-part series, SENG President Lori Comallie-Caplan and Marc Caplan guide parents through the difficult topic of helping their gifted children through divorce. SENG Director Marianne Kuzujanakis writes from personal experience about the role of a pediatric doctor in the care of gifted children, and Sheri Plybon, also a SENG Director, shares her thoughts on moving toward self-actualization.

The final section, "First Person Gifted," is a collection of personal stories from a variety of viewpoints about the experience of being gifted in a world that is not always understanding of differences. Former SENG President Rosina M. Gallagher offers stories of resilient Hispanic women, SENG Director Tiombe-Bisa Kendrick writes about the hardships of being gifted within culturally diverse populations, and SENG Director Vidisha Patel shares her own experience of the joys and challenges of Indian immigrant families. A profile of

Jeremy Tardy, an acting student at Juilliard, shows what it takes to fulfill one's dreams, and Angela Arenivar writes about being "under the spell of words" and her experience in the Scripps National Spelling Bee. A mother and son writing team, Holly and Joseph Hughes, write about their story of how giftedness can be misunderstood, especially when children do not achieve in traditional ways. SENG Director Lisa Rivero shares perspectives on why her family chose to homeschool, and Michael Postma writes of his experience of being the father of a child who both is gifted and has Asperger's Syndrome. The last essay is a personal perspective on coming to terms with being a gifted adult, by Helen Prince.

We would like to thank these and all of the fine contributors to SENG's newsletters and online library throughout the years. Your words make a real difference in the lives of gifted children and adults around the world.

2012 SENG Board of Directors

President: Lori Comallie-Caplan
President-Elect: Sheri Plybon
Finance Officer: Vidisha Patel
Secretary: Tiombe Kendrick
Rose Blackett
Kathleen Casper
Jane Hesslein
Carolyn Kottmeyer
Marianne Kuzujanakis
Joy Navan
Tiffany O'Neill
Lisa Rivero
Executive Director: Elizabeth Campbell

PART I

The SENG Difference

Coming Full Circle

by Jane Hesslein

I am part of a very small group of people on the planet who have been connected with SENG for nearly all of its existence; I'm a SENG lifer. Considering how quickly organizations come and go today, that's a pretty remarkable statement. SENG has enriched my abilities as a parent and my career as a teacher.

When the review of *Guiding the Gifted Child* (Webb, Meckstroth, and Tolan) was published in *The Wall Street Journal* in 1982, my father carefully clipped it out and mailed it to me with a note that said simply: "You need this book."

At the time, my husband and I had two young children and lived in Scarborough, Ontario. Josh was in first grade, a budding paleontologist specializing in trilobites; Annie was in preschool, discovering the world's patterns and making friends from around the world.

I loved that book. If I had a question after reading it, I knew that if I just carried the book with me long enough, the answer would come to me. The book had answers to questions I hadn't even asked. I hadn't thought of my kids as gifted, but the authors certainly had them pegged. Somehow my dad had known that.

A few years later, as the president of the parent group at

Josh's school, I ordered 20 copies of the book to sell as a fund-raiser. Jim Webb's autograph, which I thought was a bold request on my part, made the books more valuable. Parents snapped them up.

I began to attend the SENG conferences, considering them my summer camp. I attended alone, with the idea that this was my weekend to feed both the mind and the heart. Anytime I sat down, my question "What brought you here?" started great conversations and lovely friendships. Some of what I learned was for my kids; some of it was for me. And much of it was for my students, since I was now taking courses in gifted education and providing gifted programming.

In the late 1980's, I took the SMPG training given by Jim Webb and Arlene DeVries, and I began leading parent groups in the Minneapolis area. I had such a good time that I did the training again in 1992. When I signed up the third time, Jim and Arlene asked me to present with them, as a point person for local resources. Maybe they were just being sure they had space for other attendees. (Maybe now they'll tell me.)

In 1995, I had a request to present the training, which Jim encouraged. Around then, I also started presenting at SENG conferences, which led to presentations at other state and national conferences. Each time, my topic had a strong social/emotional piece. I'm not sure it would have been so clear to me to include that facet without my SENG training.

Now I'm on SENG's Board of Directors. I'm excited and humbled to think of continuing the organization's mission and vision.

This organization has had a tremendous effect on me, my children, my students, and their parents. It has touched anyone who has heard me present. The skills that I learned as a parent group facilitator are in use every day that I teach.

Whether I'm working with students, parents, school administrators, or local resources, the background that my training provided has given me a foundation like no other.

I encourage parents and teachers to attend a SENG conference. I wish more teachers would consider the training. Even if they don't ever facilitate a group, the parents they deal with would benefit on a daily basis from what they'd learn.

Recently, I had the opportunity to say to my son, "You need this book."

I've come full-circle. Thanks, Dad. This year's donation is in your memory.

Jane Hesslein's professional orientation has focused on gifted children from the beginning. Currently teaching fifth grade Humanities at Seattle Country Day School (an independent school for the gifted), her career has also taken her to public and private settings in New Jersey, Texas, Ontario, and Minnesota. A SENG Model Parent Group facilitator since 1989, Jane's goal is to promote SENG awareness and sensibilities among the teachers and families of the gifted.

SENG's 25th Anniversary Conference:

Reflections on SENG's History

By James T. Webb

I n August 1980, a very bright, talented 17 year old Dallas Egbert, from Dayton, Ohio, committed suicide. His parents contacted me, as a child psychologist, to inquire whether there were any programs that focused on the social and emotional needs of gifted children and their families. It soon became apparent that despite a clear need, few resources existed.

It was from this tragedy that SENG began, and today I am happy to say that SENG and its many programs—indeed its very existence—have touched the lives of thousands of gifted children and their families in positive ways. Now, more than 25 years later, we look back on an interesting history—and forward to an even more interesting future.

Many people now take SENG's existence for granted, but it was not always that way and many people have been key in determining SENG's growth. SENG started in 1980 as part of the School of Professional Psychology at Wright State University, thanks to the wisdom and support of the Dean, Ronald Fox (elected president of the American Psychological Association in 1994) who protected SENG from faculty members who believed that programs for gifted children and their families had little relevance for psychologists. In January 1981, television talk show personality Phil Donahue hosted a show about gifted children and depression. I participated in that show, along with Dr. and Mrs. Egbert, Jean and Bill Casey (parents of a gifted son who had also committed suicide), several other families, and Joyce Juntune, who was then the Executive Director of the National Association for Gifted Children. To everyone's amazement, that edition of "The Donahue Show" resulted in 20,000 calls and letters from people across the country confirming the extent of neglect, misunderstanding, and prevalence of myths regarding gifted children and their families.

This outpouring from viewers caused those of us involved with SENG to redouble our efforts. We wanted to increase the awareness of parents, teachers and others working with gifted children, and to help them realize that these children and their families do have special emotional needs and opportunities that are often overlooked and, thus, neglected. Sometimes, the result is underachievement or unrealized potential; but sometimes the outcome is misery and depression.

Following the Donahue Show, Betty Meckstroth, a parent, volunteered her time and energy. She and I initiated SENG parent support groups—a series of guided discussions focusing on ten major topics of concern to parents. We provided basic written material noting key points relevant to the topic, encouraged parents to express their concerns, and offered professional comment, advice, discussion, and guidance. As the parents shared ideas and experiences, they learned from each other—lessons such as how to appreciate and encourage each child, how to anticipate problems and find solutions, and how to prevent difficulties. We are deeply indebted to those parents for their sharing, courage and support; we probably learned as much from them as they did from us. These parent group sessions eventually resulted in the book, *Guiding the Gifted Child*, and later *Gifted Parent Groups: The SENG Model*. The parent support groups continue to be a hallmark of SENG.

Another early aspect of SENG was consultation with psychologists, teachers, and other professionals individually and through workshops. It quickly became apparent that professionals lack useful training in characteristics and needs of gifted children—an unfortunate situation that continues to this day.

Thanks to Betty Meckstroth's efforts, the Junior League of Dayton provided seed money and volunteers that allowed us to hold the First Annual SENG Conference in 1982. We invited speakers from across the country; and to our amazement, they came. In a few short years, the SENG program gradually developed a reputation as a support system for gifted children and their families, as well as for educators interested in the emotional and social concerns of gifted children. SENG began to receive national media coverage, including interviews and commentary from *Good Morning America, CBS Sunday Morning, National Public Radio,* and *CNN.*

As is often the case, a program does not develop smoothly. Funding was—and continues to be—a problem. However, miracles do happen, sometimes in surprising ways. The owner of a Bingo game discovered that, for tax reasons, he needed to give money to a charity, and SENG became the grateful beneficiary of his donation. These funds allowed SENG to hire staff and underwrite programs for several years. Then, just as this funding waned, a new and very special donor appeared and continued SENG's funding because she remembered how she, as a very bright girl in New York City, had suffered from discrimination and lack of support for her talent and abilities. This donor was Eugenie Radney from Akron, Ohio. Eugenie donated money while she was alive, and bequeathed money from her estate that SENG received when she died.

In the years from 1981 through 1993, SENG continued to hold annual conferences, train psychologists, and conduct parent support groups. With help from people like Arlene DeVries, of Des Moines, Iowa, others around the country were trained in the SENG parent support group model. For three years, 1986-1989, AAGC (the American Association for Gifted Children) merged with SENG, thanks to the efforts of AAGC President Anne Impellizzeri, and SENG was involved in working with the Presidential Scholars program in Washington, DC.

In 1994, when I knew that I would be leaving Wright State University, we moved SENG to Kent State University where Dr. Jim Delisle and Dr. Joanne Rand Whitmore—both national leaders in the social and emotional needs of gifted children— were faculty members. A few years later, we decided that it made more sense for SENG to become its own entity, independent of any university setting.

In the year 2000, a SENG National Advisory Committee of people who were knowledgeable and representative in the field of gifted education was established to decide SENG's future direction. Committee members were: Dr. Ed Amend, Raenele Côté, Arlene DeVries, Carolyn Kottmeyer, Sharon Lind, Dr. Rick Olenchak, Dr. Joanne Whitmore Schwartz, and Dr. James Webb. This committee became SENG's first board of directors and decided that SENG should apply for official non-profit 501(c) (3) status. Thanks to Board President Sharon Lind's dedicated efforts, SENG achieved non-profit status in 2001.

As SENG celebrates its 25th "Silver Anniversary"

Conference, the organization shows promise of being even more active in fulfilling its mission to educate others about the needs of gifted children. Recent SENG accomplishments and programs currently being developed include:

- Continuing Education credits for psychologists (offered at all SENG conferences since 2002 and home study courses currently in development)
- Establishment of a National Professional Advisory Committee in 2005
- A DVD on issues of misdiagnosis and dual diagnoses of gifted children
- A brochure (developed jointly with NAGC in 2007) about gifted children to be distributed to all pediatricians and family practitioners in the U.S.
- Establishment of *SENG Nos Apoya*, a program with emphasis on special needs of Hispanic parents of gifted children, currently in development
- Hiring our first Executive Director, Amy Price, in March 2007
- Establishment of *The SENG Honor Roll*, to provide national and local recognition to educators making a difference for gifted children
- Designating National Parenting Gifted Children Week, the third week of July of each year since 2008.

I hope this information about the history of SENG will prompt you to support SENG's efforts, both financially and emotionally. Most of all, I hope you will register to attend a SENG conference. You will meet many of the people mentioned above, and others, who have helped SENG grow and develop to what it is today. Our continuing goal is to help gifted children and their families not only to obtain important knowledge, but also to understand and accept themselves and others in ways that value, nurture, and support them in families, schools, workplaces, and communities.

Dr. James T. Webb established the SENG (Supporting Emotional Needs of Gifted Children) at Wright State University's School of Professional Psychology in 1981. This led to the publication of the award-winning book, Guiding the Gifted Child, *and later,* Gifted Parent Groups: The SENG Model. *Dr. Webb is president of Great Potential Press, an award-winning publisher of books for parents and teachers of gifted children. He has been recognized as one of the 25 most influential psychologists nationally on gifted education in a national survey published in* Gifted Child Today.

SMPG: My Gifted Education

By Carol Raymond

Several years ago, I enrolled in my first graduate course in gifted education – "The Social and Emotional Needs of Gifted Learners." At that point, I did not have plans to continue an advanced degree in gifted education; I simply sought to understand my eldest stepdaughter better. I yearned for answers to her questions and solutions to her problems.

Through my graduate work, I developed answers to some of the questions she had as an adolescent, but as I grew, so did she, and she can still pose questions to which I have no answers, and those solutions to her problems that I might suggest are often ignored in her stubborn pursuit of her own independent solutions.

However, the education I received opened my eyes to the importance of the field of gifted education while also shedding light on many of my own idiosyncrasies and lifelong struggles.

After my own personal revelations, I desired to share all I knew about giftedness and gifted children with others. As a gifted specialist, I attended numerous parent-teacher conferences and heard many similar questions and concerns. I began offering courses for parents and quickly saw this parent education transform the understanding of giftedness at my school. Participants shared their new insight with other parents which incited a paradigm shift within the school community. I was hungry for more and was thrilled to attend the SENG Model Parent Group (SMPG) training and become an SMPG facilitator.

The SMPG sessions continued to make a difference within the gifted community in my area. Many of the individuals involved in the sessions became strong, educated advocates for gifted programs within our area school districts. More importantly, they became advisors and counselors to other parents of gifted children. After witnessing such positive effects of the groups, I became eager to see the SMPG grow in size and influence. This desire led me to a nationwide research project measuring the effectiveness of the SMPG on parent attitudes and the understanding of giftedness. I was anxious to see if the changes that I witnessed within my group were constant throughout the nation.

Although the SENG-Model parent group concept was conceived in 1981 and thousands of parents have participated, no formal study has been carried out to document this model's effectiveness. This study aimed to add quantitative data to support the SENG-model parent group's success.

At the time of the study's inception (Fall 2009), the SENG website listed 128 trained facilitators in 25 states and three countries (United States, Australia and France). All facilitators received an electronic invitation with information about the study's goals. Thirteen facilitators agreed to participate in the study. Twenty-six participants from three states (Texas, Kentucky and Utah) completed the Pre-SMPG survey in the Fall of 2009. Sixteen participants completed the Post-SMPG survey following the 10 week study.

The survey questions focused on five areas: gifted characteristics, unique social and emotional needs, peer and family relationships, discipline issues, educational concerns, and advocacy. Four individuals completed a follow-up phone interview.

Understanding Gifted Characteristics

Participants expressed an increase in their understanding of the gifted characteristics of their children. One participant stated "I went in not understanding a thing about gifted children. Now I feel I have a much better understanding of my child and of other gifted children, and an educated awareness of his needs."

In a follow-up interview, one parent of two children, ages eight and nine, discussed how she entered the group thinking that only one of her children demonstrated "true" gifted characteristics. Through the SMPG, she discovered the wide range of gifted characteristics and the unique manifestations of different combinations of these characteristics. She realized that both children, though extremely different, displayed typical characteristics of gifted individuals. Another interviewee who entered the study with a solid understanding of giftedness shared her discovery of the "nuances" of gifted characteristics.

Understanding Unique Social and Emotional Needs

The survey results showed a better understanding of characteristics such as "asynchronous development" and "twice-exceptional." Parents reported that they gained insight on important questions to ask when choosing a mental healthcare professional. Participants also showed marked growth in utilizing effective strategies to assist children with stress management.

In follow up interviews, parents shared stories of vast

improvement in the understanding of their child's social and emotional needs, as well as their ability to meet these unique needs. One parent stated "I feel better about things. I was ready to put my daughter in counseling because I couldn't understand the temper tantrums at age 9, but now I patiently sit and talk with her and work things out...I think she will be fine."

Another mother expressed that the SMPG "helped [her] to see better ways to help [her] child's emotional needs." Parents expressed different approaches and strategies that they had learned which had benefitted their child's social and emotional development.

Attitudes toward Peer and Family Relationships

Many parents entered the SMPG due to their child's difficulties in relationships either within their families or with peers.

Through the study, parents gained a better understanding of their own giftedness and the importance of self-understanding while parenting gifted individuals. One parent remembers, "I think it has just made us a little more relaxed about it all. He's a good kid, but you can get lost in all the issues that you can lose sight of that and think 'Oh we're failing miserably' or 'we have some serious problems here.' It's helped us chill out."

Another parent commented on the helpful strategies discussed for assistance with discipline issues with strong willed children. "I took away many [strategies from the group], but mostly how to view my child's behavior and the reasons behind it. Instead of reacting quickly and without thinking, I try to think about what is motivating him and respond accordingly. I also try to listen more and ask questions differently so that I'm able to be a better listener."

Attitudes about Educational Concerns

Though the SPMG primarily focuses on social and emotional concerns within gifted children, many parents gained confidence in their ability to advocate for their gifted child within the educational setting. Parents recognized that a good education "fit" will consequently improve their child's social and emotional wellbeing. Participants grasped educational terminology as well as strategies necessary for advocating for their child. One parent stated, "I really knew nothing of giftedness before the group and now feel comfortable advocating for my child."

The results of this study show a positive growth within parental attitudes and an understanding of giftedness. After attending the sessions, the parents reported a gain of confidence in their ability to meet the unique needs of their gifted children and recognized unique gifted characteristics within their children. Many parents commented about how they had never had a place before where they could honestly share their concerns about their children – concerns which seemed foreign to the same-age children of their peers. Gifted parents often suffer the same types of isolation that gifted students face. Often, it appears that no advice exists for the unique characteristics and circumstances of their child (Geiger, 1997). The SMPG served as the "safe" place they had not previously experienced. Outside of the SMPG, others often construed the participants concerns as "bragging" or "unreal problems."

However, within the group, parents validated each other's concerns. They relished in the environment where peers understood and empathized with their frustrations. Many appreciated the conversations with parents of older children who had experienced similar issues. These timeless conversations helped parents realize their children would "be alright" in the end.

Parents also gained a wide variety of tips and tools for advocating for their child's needs within the school system. Instead of fearing their contact with the schools, the SPMG encourages a partnership with educational institutions. This collaboration increases the likelihood of a wholesome educational experience for both the child and the parent. A positive educational environment greatly benefits the social and emotional needs of the gifted child.

One significant benefit of the SMPG is the realization and acceptance of the parents' own giftedness. "Appreciating differences in children starts with parents appreciating their own differences" (Meckstroth, 1990, "Gifted Parents," para. 1). Most mothers enter the group saying that their child "got their smarts from their dad." Many parents admit that they still experience frustration with colleagues and peers who "don't get them." Throughout the 10 weeks, parents gain an understanding of their own intelligence and sort out their past hurts and regrets. Parents often realize how they struggled with many of the same issues that their children currently face, and cherish strategies that help their child avoid some of the difficulties that they encountered.

Where do we go from here?

A further longitudinal study regarding the success and benefits of the SPMG must be completed in the future.

To enlarge the sample size, Pre-SMPG and Post-SMPG should be collected over multiple years with additional participants. If you are a facilitator, please consider future involvement.

Positive interaction between schools and parents enhances

student success. The awareness of the unique gifted characteristics, gifted terminology, and potential difficulties that the SPMG imparts empowers parents in their pursuit of educational excellence as well as social and emotional stability for their child. Districts should reach out to SENG to create SMPG programs within their district. Whether district supported, grant funded, or offered with a pass-through fee for services, a program such as the SMPG serves as a vital element for a successful gifted program. Once individuals understand the importance of the gifted program within their district, their willingness to dedicate time and finances toward the program drastically increases. A SMPG can foster mentorships, community partnerships, and volunteerism within the local school district.

For many, attending an SMPG serves as an awakening, much like my experience in my first graduate class. Parents often enter the first session looking for advice and "quick fixes" for pressing issues with their precocious children. Months later, they leave with a greater understanding of giftedness and quite frequently gain a renewed self-awareness. The readings, facilitators and other parents offer fabulous tips and strategies, but no strategy, no matter how great, can "solve" the puzzle of a gifted child! Parents learn to accept and appreciate the complex structure of their gifted child. Let's work together to grow the SENG Model Parent Groups and empower parents of gifted children with this life-changing experience.

References

Geiger, R. (1997). Meeting the needs of the highly gifted: A parent's perspective. *Roeper Review, 19*(3), 6-9.

Meckstroth, E. (1990). Parents' role in encouraging highly gifted children. *Roeper Review, 12*(3), 208-210.

Carol M. Raymond, M.Ed. currently teaches sixth grade and leads SENG parent groups in the Dallas/Fort Worth area. She has served as a gifted and talented specialist, classroom teacher, elementary music specialist, and private music instructor/performer. Mrs. Raymond enjoys advocating for gifted individuals whether through professional development workshops, conference presentations, and parent seminars. Her gifted and twice exceptional step-daughters have largely influenced her passion for gifted education.

What SENG Means to Me:

Perspectives from

SENG's First Executive Director

By Amy Price

This is a very personal account of how SENG improved my life and that of my family. I found SENG during a desperate internet search where I was seeking solutions for my gifted, "un-thriving" son. At the time, in 2003, there were only handful of articles and resources posted on the SENG website. Each one was a gem. I devoured the information and reached out to several of the links provided on the site – to my astonishment, when I reached out to SENG, its leaders reached back. I will always be grateful to the experts that cared enough to guide me in how to understand and support my children.

During one of those first contacts, it was recommended that my family attend the SENG Conference – I think I recall it was going to be held in St. Louis that year. I didn't attend. It seemed like a big investment for something I didn't know would really make a difference. And, truth be told, I was intimidated. I knew my son was "gifted," but I didn't know if he or I would fit in with "real" gifted folks. Several years and many thousands of dollars (some spent on well-intentioned-but-not helpful services) later, I realize how much more quickly we could have improved our situation had I understood that the SENG Conference was exactly right for families like mine.

Late in 2006, SENG posted a "help wanted" ad for a new position. SENG's board was seeking its first executive director. At that time, I was executive director of an education foundation, and I loved my job, but I could not resist the lure of helping SENG reach out to others. The final interview bears mention here: Imagine entering a conference room filled with the people who had written the articles and books that had already changed your life! These "heroes" introduced themselves individually (as if I didn't already recognize them from their bios on the books I'd devoured!). I found them to be humble, genuine and truly one of the most committed groups of professionals that I'd ever encountered. I became SENG's first executive director early in 2007. Five years later, I have an even greater respect for the vision and integrity of this organization and its hard working volunteer board and committees.

There have been so many "aha" moments for me over the past years. Here are just a few things I've learned from SENG:

- I'm not alone – and neither are you. SENG is a welcoming community of parents, educators, health professionals and gifted adults just like you and me.
- Our fears and frustrations are not unique. Even the gifted experts have experienced those same challenges and uncertainties in raising their own families. Often, that's why they are so dedicated to SENG and to the thousands of people worldwide that utilize SENG's services.
- Like many of you, my own expectations and demands

for change for my son were always born of concern, but often they were not effective. I did not expect that the greatest gift SENG would provide was a new perspective that allowed me to better served my loved ones – and me!

For the past five years I had the privilege of receiving SENG phone calls and emails from people around the world that were seeking answers to help themselves, their families and their students and patients. It has been the greatest pleasure to get to know so many passionate, caring people and, many times, to receive feedback about how SENG has changed lives in truly wonderful ways.

SENG lives up to its name as "Supporting Emotional Needs of the Gifted," and there is no doubt that I got more than I expected from my personal and professional involvement with SENG. I hope that my personal history with SENG serves as a catalyst for others who are just beginning their journey to better understand themselves and their loved ones. And if SENG has already made a difference in your life, I encourage you to share your story at http://www.sengifted.org/getting-involved/what-seng-means-to-me so that others who find this wonderful organization will know more quickly that they have truly found their community.

_____

As SENG's first executive director, Amy Price recognized the importance of sharing SENG's mission and vision worldwide. Her business and marketing leadership helped SENG to expand its primary programs, develop and launch new programs, and extend services to people in all 50 U.S. states and over 20 countries. Prior to joining the SENG team, Amy was Executive Director of a public school education foundation.

Part II

Understanding Giftedness

Overexcitability and the Gifted

By Sharon Lind

A small amount of definitive research and a great deal of naturalistic observation have led to the belief that intensity, sensitivity and overexcitability are primary characteristics of the highly gifted. These observations are supported by parents and teachers who notice distinct behavioral and constitutional differences between highly gifted children and their peers. The work of Kazimierz Dabrowski, (1902-1980), provides an excellent framework with which to understand these characteristics. Dabrowski, a Polish psychiatrist and psychologist, developed the Theory of Positive Disintegration as a response to the prevalent psychological theories of his time. He believed that conflict and inner suffering were necessary for advanced development – for movement towards a hierarchy of values based on altruism – for movement from "what is" to "what ought to be." Dabrowski also observed that not all people move towards an advanced level of development but that innate ability/intelligence combined with overexcitability (OE) were predictive of potential for higher-level development. It is important to emphasize that not all gifted or highly gifted individuals have overexcitabilities. However we do find more people with OEs in the gifted population than in the average population.

Overexcitabilities

Overexcitabilities are inborn intensities indicating a heightened ability to respond to stimuli. Found to a greater degree in creative and gifted individuals, overexcitabilities are expressed in increased sensitivity, awareness, and intensity, and represent a real difference in the fabric of life and quality of experience. Dabrowski identified five areas of intensity- Psychomotor, Sensual, Intellectual, Imaginational, and Emotional. A person may possess one or more of these. "One who manifests several forms of overexcitability, sees reality in a different, stronger and more multisided manner" (Dabrowski, 1972, p. 7). Experiencing the world in this unique way carries with it great joys and sometimes great frustrations. The joys and positives of being overexcitable need to be celebrated. Any frustrations or negatives can be positively dealt with and used to help facilitate the child's growth. The five OEs are described below. Each description is followed by several examples of strategies, which represent a fraction of the possible solutions to issues that may cause concern for overexcitable individuals or those who work and live with them. These should serve as a springboard for brainstorming additional strategies or interventions that will help improve the lives of overexcitable people.

Psychomotor Overexcitabilities

Psychomotor OE is a heightened excitability of the neuromuscular system. This Psychomotor intensity includes a "capacity for being active and energetic" (Piechowski, 1991, p. 287), love of movement for its own sake, surplus of energy demonstrated by rapid speech, zealous enthusiasm, intense physical activity, and a need for action (Dabrowski & Piechowski, 1977; Piechowski, 1979, 1991). When feeling emotionally tense, individuals strong in Psychomotor OE may talk compulsively, act impulsively, misbehave and act out, display nervous habits, show intense drive (tending towards "workaholism"), compulsively organize, or become quite competitive. They derive great joy from their boundless physical and verbal enthusiasm and activity, but others may find them overwhelming. At home and at school, these children seem never to be still. They may talk constantly. Adults and peers want to tell them to sit down and be quiet! The Psychomotor OE child has the potential of being misdiagnosed as Attention Deficit Hyperactivity Disorder (ADHD).

Psychomotor Strategies

- Allow time for physical or verbal activity, before, during, and after normal daily and school activities-these individuals love to "do" and need to "do." Build activity and movement into their lives.
- Be sure the physical or verbal activities are acceptable and not distracting to those around them. This may take some work, but it can be a fun project and beneficial to all.
- Provide time for spontaneity and open-ended, freewheeling activities. These tend to favor the needs of a person high in Psychomotor OE.

Sensual Overexcitability

Sensual OE is expressed as a heightened experience of sensual pleasure or displeasure emanating from sight, smell, touch, taste, and hearing (Dabrowski & Piechowski, 1977; Piechowski, 1979, 1991). Those with Sensual OE have a far more expansive experience from their sensual input than the average person. They have an increased and early appreciation of aesthetic pleasures such as music, language, and art, and derive endless delight from tastes, smells, textures, sounds, and sights. But because of this increased sensitivity, they may also feel over stimulated or uncomfortable with sensory input. When emotionally tense, some individuals high in Sensual OE may overeat, go on buying sprees, or seek the physical sensation of being the center of attraction (Dabrowski & Piechowski, 1977; Piechowski, 1979, 1991). Others may withdraw from stimulation. Sensually overexcitable children may find clothing tags, classroom noise, or smells from the cafeteria so distracting that schoolwork becomes secondary. These children may also become so absorbed in their love of a particular piece of art or music that the outside world ceases to exist.

Sensual Strategies

- Whenever possible, create an environment which limits offensive stimuli and provides comfort.
- Provide appropriate opportunities for being in the limelight by giving unexpected attention, or facilitating creative and dramatic productions that have an audience. These individuals literally feel the recognition that comes from being in the limelight.
- Provide time to dwell in the delight of the sensual and to create a soothing environment.

Intellectual Overexcitability

Intellectual OE is demonstrated by a marked need to seek understanding and truth, to gain knowledge, and to analyze and synthesize (Dabrowski & Piechowski, 1977; Piechowski, 1979, 1991). Those high in Intellectual OE have incredibly active minds. They are intensely curious, often avid readers, and usually keen observers. They are able to concentrate, engage in prolonged intellectual effort, and are tenacious in problem solving when they choose. Other characteristics may include relishing elaborate planning and having remarkably detailed visual recall. People with Intellectual OE frequently love theory, thinking about thinking, and moral thinking. This focus on moral thinking often translates into strong concerns about moral and ethical issues-fairness on the playground, lack of respect for children, or being concerned about "adult" issues such as the homeless, AIDS, or war. Intellectually overexcitable people are also quite independent of thought and sometimes appear critical of and impatient with others who cannot sustain their intellectual pace. Or they may be become so excited about an idea that they interrupt at inappropriate times.

Intellectual Strategies

- Show how to find the answers to questions. This respects and encourages a person's passion to analyze, synthesize, and seek understanding.
- Provide or suggest ways for those interested in moral and ethical issues to act upon their concerns-such as collecting blankets for the homeless or writing to soldiers in Kosovo. This enables them to feel that they can help, in even a small way, to solve community or worldwide problems.
- If individuals seem critical or too outspoken to others, help them to see how their intent may be perceived as cruel or disrespectful. For example saying "that is a stupid idea" may not be well received, even if the idea is truly stupid.

Imaginational Overexcitability

Imaginational OE reflects a heightened play of the imagination with rich association of images and impressions, frequent use of image and metaphor, facility for invention and fantasy, detailed visualization, and elaborate dreams (Dabrowski & Piechowski, 1977; Piechowski, 1979, 1991). Often children high in Imaginational OE mix truth with fiction, or create their own private worlds with imaginary companions and dramatizations to escape boredom. They find it difficult to stay tuned into a classroom where creativity and imagination are secondary to learning rigid academic curriculum. They may write stories or draw instead of doing seatwork or participating in class discussions, or they may have difficulty completing tasks when some incredible idea sends them off on an imaginative tangent.

Imaginational Strategies

- Imaginational people may confuse reality and fiction because their memories and new ideas become blended in their mind. Help individuals to differentiate between their imagination and the real world by having them place a stop sign in their mental videotape, or write down or draw the factual account before they embellish it.
- Help people use their imagination to function in the real world and promote learning and productivity. For example, instead of the conventional school organized notebook, have children create their own organizational system.

Emotional Overexcitability

Emotional OE is often the first to be noticed by parents. It is reflected in heightened, intense feelings, extremes of complex emotions, identification with others' feelings, and strong affective expression (Piechowski, 1991). Other manifestations include physical responses like stomachaches and blushing or concern with death and depression (Piechowski, 1979). Emotionally overexcitable people have a remarkable capacity for deep relationships; they show strong emotional attachments to people, places, and things (Dabrowski & Piechowski, 1977). They have compassion, empathy, and sensitivity in relationships. Those with strong Emotional OE are acutely aware of their own feelings, of how they are growing and changing, and often carry on inner dialogs and practice self-judgment (Piechowski, 1979, 1991). Children high in Emotional OE, are often accused of "overreacting." Their compassion and concern for others, their focus on relationships, and the intensity of their feelings may interfere with everyday tasks like homework or doing the dishes.

Emotional Strategies

- Accept all feelings, regardless of intensity. For people who are not highly emotional, this seems particularly odd. They feel that those high in Emotional OE are just being melodramatic. But if we accept their emotional intensity and help them work through any problems that might result, we will facilitate healthy growth.

- Teach individuals to anticipate physical and emotional responses and prepare for them. Emotionally intense people often don't know when they are becoming so overwrought that they may lose control or may have physical responses to their emotions. Help them to identify the physical warning signs of their emotional stress such as headache, sweaty palms, and stomachache. By knowing the warning signs and acting on them early, individuals will be better able to cope with emotional situations and not lose control.

General Strategies

It is often quite difficult and demanding to work and live with overexcitable individuals. Those who are not so, find the behaviors unexplainable, frequently incomprehensible, and often bizarre. Overexcitable people living with other overexcitable people often have more compassion and understanding for each other, but may feel conflicts when their OEs are not to the same degree. Finding strategies for helping children and adults deal with and take advantage of these innate and enduring characteristics may seem difficult. However, resources may be gathered from varied places: Literature regarding counseling, learning styles, special education, and classroom management; parenting books; even popular business texts. Perhaps the best place to begin is with the following general strategies, applicable regardless of which OEs are present.

Discuss the concept of overexcitability.

Share the descriptions of OEs with the family, class, or counseling group. Ask individuals if they see themselves with some of the characteristics. Point out that this article and many others like it indicates that being overexcitable is OK and it is understood and accepted.

Focus on the positives.

Jointly discuss the positives of each overexcitability when you first introduce the concept, and continue to point out these merits. Benefits include being energetic, enthusiastic, sensual,

38

aesthetic, curious, loyal, tenacious, moral, metacognitive, integrative, creative, metaphorical, dramatic, poetic, compassion-ate, empathetic, and self-aware.

Cherish and celebrate diversity.

One outcome of the pursuit of educational and societal equity has been a diminishing of the celebration of diversity and individual differences. Highly gifted individuals, because of their uniqueness, can fall prey to the public and personal belief that they are not OK. It is vital when discussing OEs that individuals realize that overexcitability is just one more description of who they are, as is being tall, or Asian, or left-handed. Since OEs are inborn traits, they cannot be unlearned! It is therefore exceedingly important that we accept our overexcitable selves, children, and friends. This acceptance provides validation and helps to free people from feelings of "weirdness" and isolation

Another way to show acceptance is to provide opportunities for people to pursue their passions. This shows respect for their abilities and intensities and allows time for them to "wallow" in what they love, to be validated for who they are. Removing passions as consequences for inappropriate behavior has a negative effect by giving the message that your passions, the essence of who you are, are not valuable or worthy of respect.

Use and teach clear verbal and nonverbal communication skills.

All people deserve respect and need to be listened to and responded to with grace. Overexcitable people need this under-standing and patience to a greater degree because they are experiencing the world with greater intensity and need to be able to share their intensity and feelings of differentness to

39

thrive. It is vital to learn good communication skills and to teach them to children. Good communication skills are useful on multiple levels, from improving the chances of getting what you want, to nurturing and facilitating growth in others. Regardless of one's motivation for learning these skills, the outcomes will include less stress, greater self-acceptance, greater understanding from and about others, and less daily friction at home, school, work, or in the grocery store.

When learning communication skills be sure to include both verbal-listening, responding, questioning, telephoning, problem solving (Faber and Mazlish, 1980), and nonverbal-rhythm and use of time, interpersonal distance and touch, gestures and postures, facial expressions, tone of voice, and style of dress (Nowicki, 1992). Verbal and nonverbal strategies improve interpersonal communication and provide the skills individuals need to fit in when they wish to, to change the system if necessary, and to treat others with caring and respect.

Teach stress management from toddlerhood on.

Everyone deals with stress on a daily basis. But overexcitable individuals have increased stress reactions because of their increased reception of and reaction to external input. There are many programs and books about stress reduction. The key components are to (1) learn to identify your stress symptoms: headache, backache, pencil tapping, pacing, etc. (2) develop strategies for coping with stress: talk about your feelings, do relaxation exercises, change your diet, exercise, meditate, ask for help, develop organizational and time management skills and (3) develop strategies to prevent stress: make time for fun; develop a cadre of people to help, advise, humor you; practice tolerance of your own and others' imperfections.

Create a comforting learning environment whenever possible.

Intense people need to know how to make their environment more comfortable in order to create places for retreat or safety. For example: find places to work or think which are not distracting, work in a quiet or calm environment, listen to music, look at a lovely picture, carry a comforting item, move while working, or wear clothing which does not scratch or cling. Learning to finesse one's environment to meet one's needs takes experimentation and cooperation from others, but the outcome will be a greater sense of well being and improved productivity.

Help to raise awareness of one's behaviors and their impact on others.

Paradoxically, overexcitable people are often insensitive and unaware of how their behaviors affect others. They may assume that everyone will just understand why they interrupt to share an important idea, or tune out when creating a short story in their head during dinner. It is vital to teach children and adults to be responsible for their behaviors, to become more aware of how their behaviors affect others, and to understand that their needs are not more important than those of others. The key is to realize that you can show children and adults how they are perceived, you can teach them strategies to fit in, but they must choose to change.

Remember the joy.

Often when overexcitability is discussed examples and concerns are mostly negative. Remember that being overexcitable also brings with it great joy, astonishment, beauty, compassion, and creativity. Perhaps the most important thing is to acknowledge and relish the uniqueness of an overexcitable child or adult.

References

Dabrowski, K. (1972). Psychoneurosis is not an illness. London: Gryf. (Out of print)

Dabrowski, K & Piechowski, M.M. (1977). Theory of levels of emotional development (Vols.1 & 2). Oceanside, NY: Dabor Science. (Out of print)

Faber, A. & Mazlish, E. (1980). How to talk so kids will listen, and listen so kids will talk. New York: Avon.

Sharon Lind, M.S., was one of SENG's founding members and served as its first President. In her many years of service to gifted individuals and families, she has had leadership roles in several national and regional organizations and is a gifted education and parenting consultant.

Asynchronous Development

By Jean Goerss

"I don't want to be gifted, Mom! I hate school!" cried my son after a particularly hard day. What makes a child want to deny who he is?

"He has to learn to deal with all kinds of people and situations eventually. You are being over-protective." intoned the principal. "Boys will be boys, after all."

Is he right? After 10 years of investigation, I conclude, no.

Asynchronous development is the hallmark of giftedness and in a very real sense, as gifted children mature they "grow into" their intellect and become more balanced, more normal. The more extreme the intellectual advancement is; the more extreme is the asynchrony. Social and emotional development depends on the way we perceive and process information and therefore is profoundly influenced by our intellect.

An analogy may make my point clearer: The major developmental task of a 30 week fetus is to prepare for life outside the womb by putting on a layer of fat to buffer the cold and to provide sustenance while she will be learning to breastfeed. In addition, important maturation of the brain is occurring that will enable her to stabilize her body in response to changes in the environment. When these developmental milestones are achieved, she is ready to cope with the environment she will encounter outside the womb.

If, instead, she is born prematurely, thin, weak and metabolically unstable, she will suffer from her lack of preparedness. She may be unable to cope with temperature changes; she may not be able to breastfeed. She may not be ready to cope with the new environment. She may suffer physical complications that could result in handicaps. In fact, she may die without assistance. Should she go home with her mother? Is it wise to "see how it goes" before resorting to special care? After all, she has to cope with the environment eventually.

If there is a place to keep her warm and stabilize her body temperature and a method to feed her while she finishes her physical preparations for the world, she will probably thrive. Is this over-protective? Will she be dependent on these interventions for the rest of her life? Clearly not.

The major developmental task of a five year old child is to prepare for life outside his family by developing a strong sense of belonging in a world in which he is not the center of attention. He becomes comfortable among peers. Normal social development depends on his ability to identify with and bond to other individuals. This bonding prompts him to conform to minimum behavioral standards that will allow him to be effective in the larger world. A sociologist would say he must acculturate. (While it is important to develop independence, he must wait until his teens to tackle that task.) To acculturate, he must have some success in navigating and coping with expectations and he must develop an affinity for; a camaraderie with his peers.

The gifted child, because of his asynchronous development, cannot identify with the peers he finds in the local school. He usually does not share their interests and may find their behavior puzzling. He may be unable or unwilling to respond to his peers as they expect; or to conform to the school's expectations. He may not be ready to cope with this new environment and, thus he may be unable to complete a basic developmental task. If so, he will suffer social and emotional complications that could profoundly affect his future.

If there were a place to meet peers with whom he could identify, with adults who understand how to help him cope and with the intellectual stimulation he craves, he could thrive. Is this overprotective? Will he be dependent on these interventions the rest of his life?

I believe many gifted children are irreparably damaged socially and emotionally in the first few years of formal schooling. Given that the environment in which we develop has a profound, physical effect on the development of the brain, it is no less urgent that we care for a child's social and emotional health than their physical health.

Academic and personal success depend more on normal social and emotional development than on curriculum. Effective personal habits, good attitudes, social competence and emotional stability all depend on social and emotional learning and maturation. If normal social and emotional developmental tasks are not accomplished, the best curriculum in the world will not make up for the resulting handicaps.

For further reading on asynchronous development, myths about gifted children, and how to enrich your child's emotional life, search for and read these articles from SENG's online Articles Library, available at http://www.sengifted.org:

- "Competing with myths about the social and emotional development of gifted students"

- "Appropriate expectations for the gifted child"
- "Factors in the social adjustment and social acceptability of extremely gifted children"
- "Developmental phases of social development"

Dr. Goerss is a Board Certified pediatrician and a co-author of the book, Misdiagnosis and Dual Diagnoses of Gifted Children and Adults: ADHD, Bipolar, OCD, Asperger's, Depression and other Disorders. *Dr. Goerss counsels gifted families, and is a speaker on gifted-related topics such as parenting, early education, psychiatric diagnoses, and school choice.*

Young Gifted Children

By Beverly Shaklee

I am in my twenty-seventh year of teaching, having started as a first grade teacher, and later becoming a third/fourth grade teacher, a consulting teacher in gifted education, a resource teacher in gifted education, and now a university professor in gifted and teacher education. If it sounds like I keep following my passion, you would be correct, I do! One of my ongoing areas of concern, interest and research has been in young gifted children, including the children of poverty, minorities, "new Americans," and those historically underrepresented in our programs for gifted and talented children. Another, and perhaps my most important, passion has been my own gifted son – his growth, development and arrival as a healthy adult to this world.

As a parent, teacher and researcher, I am continually asked the same or similar questions from parents regarding their young gifted children:

"What should I be doing with them (or not)?"

"Should I have them tested?"

"How do I reconcile my role as parent with their giftedness (or not)?"

"What are reasonable expectations?"

"Where and when should they go to school?"

"How do I find the right teacher?"

"Do I have the skills as a parent to raise a gifted child?"

I really wish I had "the" answers to these questions, but as you've learned by now, there are no easy answers – just a series of good questions to be asked. In part, if you are the parent of a young gifted child and you are asking these questions and searching for answers you are on the right track. Space does not permit answering all of these questions and, of course, that will give me room for other Director's Corner columns in the future! However, I do want to comment on three areas: expectations, parenting, and schooling for young gifted children.

Young children in general are very complex. They are amazing in the tasks, abilities and areas that they develop in the first five to eight years of their life; some researchers estimate upwards of 80 percent of all of their deep knowledge is constructed at that time. Having a young child who is also cognitively gifted gives added dimension to that complexity. Although there are many issues that arise during this period of development, probably one of the most difficult to understand and address as a parent and teacher is the difference between aspects of a child's development that are age-appropriate and those that are developmentally advanced. Let me give you an example. A teacher was watching two young gifted children playing with a ball and the children began to loudly discuss, "Whose ball is it?" "It's mine!" "No, it's mine!" Knowing that the boys would understand, the teacher talked with them briefly about sharing and cooperation. "It's when you want us to let each other play," responded the boys. The teacher, thinking all was settled, turned instead to see one boy hit the other and yell, "But that ball is mine!" When you know that a cognitively gifted child can have social knowledge (knowledge of the rules and the ability to repeat them) but not social competence (actions that match), then you understand the dilemma. In fact, this is not at all uncommon. Gifted children's social knowledge is developmentally advanced but their social competence is age-appropriate for four-year-olds. This phenomenon occurs across physical and cognitive areas as well.

How do we address this issue with young gifted children? Should we expect that because they can intelligently articulate the "rules" that they will enact them at the same level? No, we shouldn't. We need to maintain reasonable expectations that take into account both dimensions of the young child's development. One of my dearest friends in early childhood education continually reminds me that we cannot see the world through the eyes of young children; they construct their view of the world in a way that makes sense to them. In some cases, that vision of the world is flawed, in part because of age, experiential knowledge, and exposure. Adults, parents and teachers must provide the bridge to understanding, because although sometimes we don't feel as if we are as intelligent as our gifted child, we do have age, experience, and exposure.

At the risk of challenging some assumptions, I do want to comment on the need to distinguish a child's accomplishments from parent and teacher accomplishments. We are rightfully proud of the efforts, work, and expertise that our children can demonstrate. But, sometimes adults have difficulty distinguishing the accomplishments of their children or students from their own development and accomplishments as adults, making it very difficult for young gifted children to make mistakes, take a risk, or tell an adult that they are unsure of themselves. Young gifted children are often sensitive enough to understand, without being able to articulate, that their "mistakes" become our mistakes. For example, the parent who praises only the A and doesn't praise the effort behind a solid B that was actually the harder accomplishment, or the parent who constantly parades the child's accomplishments in front of others, can make a young child think that he is only worthy of his parent's attention when he is successful, gets all A's and does something to brag about. Children need to live in a psychologically and physically healthy environment that permits age-appropriate experimentation, choices, time for play, and time for "mistakes." We call that learning. Sharing your adult pathway to life-long learning, your mistakes, and your adult accomplishments gives children the understanding that real learning is a balance of successes and not so successful experiences. It can help a young child to understand that she is loved for herself, not just for her accomplishments.

Jim Gallagher once said that all you have to do is watch them and young gifted children will tell you through their actions what they need to be doing. By and large, he was correct. As a parent or educator, when you are trying to make sound educational decisions for a young gifted child, I think there is only one real question, "In what ways will this benefit the child?" Parents are very knowledgeable about their young gifted children, however they are not always knowledgeable about educational alternatives. Teachers are knowledgeable about schools and classrooms, but they do not know your child and, sometimes, they don't know much about giftedness. In order to make sound educational decisions on behalf of your child at an early age, you need both groups in the room. Informed decisions that benefit the child are made based on patterns of evidence collected over time. Evidence may include standardized tests, parental observations at the school, opportunities for the child to visit the new classroom, or information collected in any manner of other ways. Using that information wisely is based on looking at the age-appropriate aspects of the child's development and the developmentally advanced areas; it is that delicate balance that should be considered when thinking about schooling decisions. Another decision is who will be keeping track of the early decisions made on behalf of a gifted child? Early entrance, for example, may be an option, but when the child arrives in middle school and is one or two years younger than his classmates, who accounts for that? Who ensures that the child is still getting the support they need? A long-term view is needed when we make early educational decisions on behalf of a young gifted child. Early formal schooling is not necessary to the development of giftedness or potential. Creating a literacy rich environment, time for play, informal field trips, hands-on experiences, and sound parenting, are often more useful to the development of a young gifted child than placement in a school setting.

The good news is that young gifted children are truly amazing, funny, and able to see things that we do not! Their questions are magnificent, their understandings complex, and their potential is great. Our ability to guide and nurture those gifts requires life-long learning on our part – but what a terrific adventure!

Dr. Beverly Shaklee is a Director of the Center for International Education and Professor of Curriculum and Instruction. Dr. Shaklee has a focused research agenda on the development of international educators and representation of diverse populations in gifted child education programs. She has served on the Board of Directors for SENG and the National Association for Gifted Children (NAGC), and is currently on the Board of Directors for Virginia Association for the Gifted (VAG).

Teasing and Gifted Children

By Patricia A. Schuler

"**S**hut up!" "Stop humiliating me!" "Stop it before I destroy you!" I had been observing a second grade classroom when I was jolted by these screams. Remembering these desperate words still causes chills to race up my spine. What could have triggered a boy who was peacefully reading a book to erupt into a frightening fury of anger? Teasing and taunting. After making fun of him for reading in class, the boy's classmates tattled on him. The teacher responded by taking his book away. As it turned out, the boy had been reading instead of completing work he had mastered in kindergarten.

Many gifted children and adolescents are targets of teasing and bullying. Some of their peers and teachers may perceive them as "too verbal", "too bossy", "too smart," "too nerdy." Because gifted children and adolescents tend to be highly sensitive to others, their reactions to being teased are extremely intense. One only has to look to recent shootings around the country, committed by kids who have been described as very bright, for examples of this kind of intensity.

Often the teasing and bullying is subtle- name-calling, shoving, social ostracism, or intimidation. While girls use more psychological manipulation like spreading malicious rumors, boys account for the majority of physical bullying. Too often their victims suffer in silence. Parents need to look for signs of distress: crying, not eating or sleeping during the school week, not wanting to go to school, stomachaches or headaches.

What can you as a parent do if you suspect your child is being teased or bullied? One of the first things is to help your child distinguish between harmless rough and tumble play and harmful behavior. Try to find out what is happening from your child's point of view, and accept what your child tells you as fact. Ask for specifics: Who is teasing? What does she or he do? How do you feel about it – scared, angry, hurt? What did you do about it? Did it work? Do any teachers know? What did they say or do? Offer reassurance to your child. Sharing an experience of a time when you were teased can help them understand that it is normal to be upset about what has happened. Tell them that you will help them solve this problem.

McCoy (1997) offers the following problem solving strategies that you can use when your child is teased or bullied:

1. Clarify the problem with your child.
2. Ask for other ways your child could respond the next time the situation arises. Postpone judgment: answers can be inappropriate, vindictive, silly. Include appropriate responses: walk away, be assertive, go for help.
3. Think through the consequences of each suggestion on the list and pick one to try.
4. Make a plan and try it.
5. Evaluate what happened.

What shouldn't parents do? Don't minimize the situation by suggesting that everyone gets teased. Telling children it's their problem and to stand up for themselves only makes them feel even more inadequate and powerless. Don't call the teaser and "reward" him/her with an invitation to discuss and negotiate a plan to stop the teasing by offering rewards. Don't call the teaser's parents to complain. It may make the situation worse.

Teaching gifted kids alternative strategies besides exploding in anger or suffering passively is important. In our practice, we use role-playing to explore techniques that can be used to deal with teasing. One of the first tactics is how to stay calm and ignore the situation. Counting backwards from "10 squared," or ignoring by yawning or becoming interested in something else has proven effective. Another strategy that works is self-talk. Expressions like "Calm down. I'm smart enough to handle this," or "I know what's going on and what they're trying to do. I'm not going to let them take my power away," can help a child go from being victimized to being assertive. We teach children that body language and tone of voice matter. McCoy (1997) offers suggestions on how to appear relaxed and in charge:

- Look people in the eye
- Stand up straight, with feet slightly apart
- Keep your hands in your pockets
- Move closer to the person rather than backing off as you talk
- Speak loudly enough and use a firm and determined voice

One little boy who was consistently being teased by an older girl used his "brilliant retorts" to make her really listen when he decided to be assertive. The statement, "I don't like it when people push me around," and saying something silly in a foreign language took her off guard. Doing the unexpected worked for him.

Because many gifted children and adolescents are perfectionistic, they feel that telling an adult what is happening is a reflection on their ability to control their lives. It is critical that parents tell them that informing an adult is not tattling or a measure of their abilities. Getting help from an adult is important, but they need to know when and who. Make a list with your child when he or she should run away and get help from an adult immediately (if another child threatens, hurts physically, or touches inappropriately). Say, "Try to stop their teasing or name-calling yourself, but if you can't or someone does something that makes you feel unhappy or scared, don't wait. Tell me or your teacher, so we can help you stop it" (McCoy, 1997). Who should they get help from? You or a "personal support network" at school. Make a list with your child of who these people might be. Let those on the list know that they have been selected to be part of this safety network. Ask for their assistance.

The price of being teased or bullied can be devastating. For a gifted child it may lead to intense anger, withdrawal, and/or depression. Too many suicides and murders have resulted from a bright child being teased. What can parents do? Notify your child's school immediately when your child becomes a target of teasing and bullying. Do not accept a "kids will be kids" policy. Work to have a "Zero Tolerance for Teasing" program in your school or district that includes counseling for both the victims and the bullies. More importantly, help your gifted child by providing her/him with strategies to end this pervasive and harmful practice.

Resources

McCoy, E. (1997). What to do... When kids are mean to your child. Pleasantville, NY: Reader's Digest.

Dr. Patricia Schuler is an internationally recognized speaker on the topic of the social and emotional needs of highly able students. Dr. Schuler has a Ph.D. in Educational Psychology (Gifted and Talented Education) from the University of Connecticut. She is the author of Voices of Perfectionism: Perfectionistic Gifted Adolescents in a Rural Middle School.

Sylvia Rimm on Perfectionism in the Gifted

An Interview by Michael Shaughnessy, SENG'S Editor in Chief

Question: Dr. Rimm, why does perfectionism seem to be a problem for gifted children?

Answer: Perfectionism is very close to excellence, and, of course, parents and teachers encourage excellence in children. In our great excitement at their performance, we describe their work as perfect and we award A plusses and 100 percent--all very deserving and appropriate. In fact, many gifted children go several years without the experience of making mistakes in school. Being perfect, right, and smartest easily becomes part of their persona, a persona developed by a combination of who they are and what the important adults and peers in their lives expect of them. Many talent areas demand excellence, such as music, dance, and gymnastics. Gifted children deliver this excellence, and it becomes both a good and bad habit--good when they strive for excellence; and bad when they can't tolerate mistakes or criticism, or when their fears of a less than perfect performance prevent their performing at all.

Q: Are there different types of perfectionism?

A: Yes, children can be perfectionistic in only one area, such as art or sports. Perfectionism can also become pervasive and compulsive. Some experts talk about good and bad perfectionism; others differentiate between excellence and perfectionism with the latter being problematic and the first being appropriate. If we have surgery done to us, we would like our surgeon to do it perfectly. Even when we hear a solo violinist or watch a ballet, we have come to expect perfection. Perfect shots on the basketball court score points, and so on. As you see, we have a love/hate relationship with perfectionism.

Q: Would you say perfectionism is a social or an emotional problem?

A: When perfectionism interferes with productive achievement and a happy lifestyle, it is a social and an emotional problem. For example, gifted underachievers are often, but not always, perfectionists. They view themselves as either "A" students or failures. I've heard more than one tween or teen admit to me or their parents that if they can't get A's, there is just no reason to do their work. Sometimes they don't admit this either to me or even to themselves, but you can see their motivation change as they recognize they can get A's again. Perfectionism is both a social and an emotional problem when it becomes extreme. If it is only a slight emotional problem, parents and teachers can work with it at home and in the classroom. We should always be trying to encourage excellence while preventing perfectionism, a delicate balance.

Q: How can parents and teachers best deal with a child's perfectionism?

A: There are many things that parents and teachers can do, but please don't worry if you can't do them perfectly! Here are a few:

- Praise moderately at least most of the time. Calling a child a good thinker is much better than saying he or she is the smartest or best student, is brilliant, or is a natural athlete. This is not so easy with highly gifted children, so if you slip once in a while, don't be too hard on yourself.

- Help kids feel satisfied when they have done their best, not necessarily when they have done the best compared to others.

- Read biographies together that show that successful people made mistakes and experienced failures. Emphasize the failures and rejections as well as the successes. You might ask children how they think those successful people must have felt when they were failing: discouraged, temporarily depressed, or confident and optimistic? As you think together of how others stayed motivated, your children or students can find their own solutions in dealing with their disappointments.

- Help children learn to laugh at themselves and their own mistakes, and be a model for them by laughing at some of your own mistakes or expressing your own frustration and moving forward.

[Editor's note: For more suggestions, see "What's Wrong with Perfect?" at Dr. Rimm's Web site, http://www.sylviarimm.com.]

Q: Do some children with perfectionistic tendencies require counseling?

A: When perfectionism interferes with school work, extracurricular activities, or a healthy social life, children definitely need counseling. If perfectionists exhibit symptoms of anxiety such as sleeplessness, avoidance of activities, eating disorders, or continuous headaches or stomach aches, they are likely to need counseling. Sometimes the symptoms aren't obvious, so parents and teachers must listen and observe carefully.

In counseling, we help children to learn from mistakes, set reasonable expectations of themselves and others, develop personal relaxation strategies, and and develop balance in their lives. If perfectionism is extreme, as in eating disorders or depression, counseling can become extensive and complicated.

Q: Do boys and girls have different types of perfectionistic tendencies?

A: Every study of perfectionism finds many more girls to be perfectionistic than boys. In my study of successful women for my book *See Jane Win: The Rimm Report on 100 Successful Women*, we found that more than a third of the women remembered themselves as being perfectionistic as teens. In our interviews, many of the women reported on how they had to learn to accept criticism and talk to themselves about building their self-confidence during difficult junctures in their careers.

There are also many boys who are perfectionistic. Perfectionistic boys are often helped by being involved in sports where they can learn to have plenty of mistakes and still help their teams. Encouraging kids to participate in activities which they can enjoy without being the best can help both boys and girls appreciate themselves without pressure.

Sylvia B. Rimm, PhD., is a psychologist, director of Family Achievement Clinic in Cleveland, Ohio, and a clinical professor at Case Western Reserve School of Medicine. Among her many books are How to Parent So Children Will Learn *and* Why Bright Kids Get Poor Grades, *both 2008 National Best Books award winners from* USA Book News, *and* Growing Up Too Fast, Keys to Parenting the Gifted Child, *and* See Jane Win.

Michael F. Shaughnessy is a Professor of Psychology at Eastern New Mexico University. He holds master's degrees from Bank Street College of Education and the College of New Rochelle in Guidance and Counseling and School Psychology. He has presented on gifted topics internationally and has been a Consulting Editor for Gifted Education International. *He has written, edited or co-edited about a dozen books and published several hundred articles, book reviews, research reports, interviews and commentaries.*

Can We Capture and Measure the Creativity Beast?

By Rose Blackett

According to many researchers, creativity has an elusive relationship to giftedness. Consider the part creativity plays on the stage of life, and look behind its mask. What is creativity? If we can identify the creativity beast, can we capture and measure it? A model within the New Zealand classroom context attempts to measure this elusive, socially constructed concept. Do creativity and giftedness dance a solo or a tango on the dance floor? Do they know the steps, or do they improvise?

There appears to be ongoing debate and discussion about what creativity is and how to identify and enhance it. Many question if it can measured at all. Traditionally, the *person*, *process* or *product* has been the focus in the search to capture creativity and give it meaning. Sometimes products are not accepted at a given point in time: their originality slowly emerges and is only acknowledged and appreciated by new generations. Many famous artists have died in poverty, yet their work is now considered that of a "genius."

More recent research highlights the importance of *socio-cultural factors* in defining creativity. According to Fraser (2004), creativity is an essential aspect of humanity.

Interpersonal relationships, social communication, and the context in which these interconnections occur, are now seen as building blocks for fostering creativity.

In New Zealand, Mark Dashper and the team at Te Manu Aute have been trialing a new initiative under the New Zealand Ministry of Education Talent Development Initiative. This initiative is based on a webcasting to internet model of rich media delivery of the arts to schools. Data is gathered across the arts and includes music, drama, dance, and visual arts. Teachers and students are able to view classes or presentations live (on-demand), and respond via interactive media. They access resources, and communicate and interact in a differentiated enrichment program that targets all four of the Arts for Gifted and Talented Education. This innovative program (a first, both nationally and internationally) began by attempting to define and measure creativity within the classroom context.

The schools in the trial were supplied with a selection of profiles, identification matrices, and models for identifying creativity. Schools developed their own systems for identifying creativity based on the needs of their students, current research and theory, and support from Te Manu Aute. The observation profiles developed were based on national and international publications and research.

Schools could select to use any combination of six identification tools:

- *Observation Profile and Rating Scale*, an adapted version of Jill Brandon's fifteen-point observation profile and rating scale for identifying characteristics and attitudes found in gifted and talented children in the arts.

- *Māori Differentiation Scale,* an adapted model of Jill Bevan-Brown's categories of giftedness from a Māori* perspective. This integrates a holistic Māori view of special abilities and includes concepts such as "service to others" and "traditional knowledge and skills," which are broader attributes than commonly associated with intellectually based definitions of giftedness.

- *Rating Behavioural Characteristics,* utilizing Renzulli and Hartman's scale for rating behavioral characteristics of highly creative individuals. This scale measures ability as a defined set of characteristics, and the frequency of their occurrence determines the level of an individual's skills.

- *Indicators for Creative Thinking.* Indira Neville adapted the New Zealand Council for Educational Research (NZCER) McAlpine and Reid Creative Thinking Characteristics indicators check list. Schools selected to measure descriptors such as "produces original ideas and products" as a process, through examining drafts of a students work, questions asked by students, and discussions; or as a product, based on what was produced and how original it was in form and content.

- *Performance and Submission-based Evidence.* Three forms of selection were used including portfolio assessment, authentic assessment, and self assessment opportunities.

- *Junior Observation Profile,* a profile developed specifically for the junior primary level. This profile did not separate out the arts, but was more general in the traits identified. For example, "dares to be different" and "reflective in self evaluation" were included as general characteristics. (Dashper, 2010).

67

Feedback on this initiative to date has been favorable towards the Māori Differentiation Scale and the Indicators for Creative Thinking (using the process indicators). Interestingly, many schools reported their gifted and talented students in the arts enjoyed the journey (process) more than reaching their final destination (product). Some students mastered the process early and did not necessarily want (or need) to complete a final product. The primary schools tended to favor the more generalized Junior Observation Profile, while the high schools required more subject specific measurements for individual areas of the arts. Overall, the Observation and Rating Scales were reported to be the most popular and adaptable measures in capturing the creativity beast within New Zealand classrooms in this trial.

Creativity is a difficult beast to capture precisely because it has many different manifestations, conceptions, and interpretations. As a socially constructed concept, it can be difficult to define and identify across cultures. Predicting who will be creative in adulthood from childhood traits or behaviors has proved difficult, even in retrospective studies of prodigies (Van Tassel-Baska, 2008). Research suggests *creativity and giftedness* are often interwoven and, as such, may dance a tango. Who leads this dance is very much up for debate; however, it would seem both giftedness and creativity improvise the dance as they evolve. They may even compose their own music...

If you would like further information or a copy of the profiles developed by Te Manu Aute, please visit http://www.temanuaute.org.nz.

*Māori are the indigenous people of New Zealand

References

Dashper, M. (2010). Measuring creativity in the arts. *Tall Poppies*, 35 (3), p16-17.

Fraser, D. Creativity: Shaking hands with tomorrow (2004). In D. McAlpine & R. Moltzen (Eds.), *Gifted and talented. New Zealand perspectives* (2nd ed., p145-169).

Van Tassel-Baska, J. (2008). Creativity as an elusive factor in giftedness. *Tall Poppies*, 33 (2), p31-35.

SENG Director Rose Blackett is a registered educational psychologist with over twenty years of experience in the education system. Rose is the current president of the New Zealand Association for Gifted Children (NZAGC), founding president of Christchurch Explorers and a committee member for the Canterbury Association for Gifted Education (CAGE). Rose and her husband Rob parent two gifted children and live in Christchurch.

Part III

Not Just for Parents

GT Kids and Behavior: Seven Strategies to Help Kids (and Parents) Cope

By Christine Fonseca

Gifted kids are a unique and challenging group – for teachers and for parents. They view the world through an entirely unique lens, one that is best summed up in one word. Intense. This intensity refers to how gifted individuals approach life. At its best, intensity is the driving passion that enables some people to achieve amazing things – in any domain. But at its worst, it is the turmoil that has the power to consume these same individuals from time to time as they learn how to manage that aspect of their personality.

Intensity comes in the form of cognitive intensity – those aspects of thinking and processing information that all gifted individuals use to problem solve. It relates to the attributes of focus, sustained attention, creative problem solving, and advanced reasoning skills. Most people think of cognitive intensity as intellect, or "being smart" – all good things.

But a gifted child's intensity does not stop there. The emotional aspects of a gifted individual are also intense. Emotional intensity refers to the passion gifted people feel daily. It also refers to the extreme highs and lows many gifted people experience throughout their lifetime, causing them to question their own mental stability from time to time. This type of intensity is a natural aspect of giftedness. However, in my experience, it is also one of the most misunderstood attributes – and it is the reason gifted kids sometimes struggle.

Typically, emotional intensity results in a range of behavioral outbursts that can be internal (including moodiness, anxiety, and depression) or external (yelling or crying, temper tantrums, and physical expressions of anger or frustration). Regardless of how a gifted child chooses to demonstrate his or her intensities, there are a lot of things parents and educators can do to help lessen the outburst and help teach their children and students coping strategies.

1. Start early by helping the child talk about his or her emotions. Trust me, they may not want to – but taking the emotions from some raw feeling to a tangible thing that can be defined is an important first step in learning to control the behavior. Further, the development of an emotional vocabulary can assist in providing a common language with which to discuss emotions and behavior.

2. Help the child discover his or her unique escalation cycle. Likewise, know your own. Gifted kids have considerable talent for pushing a teacher's or parent's buttons. Knowing the things that push you over the edge will enable you to remain calm during emotional outbursts, whatever form they may take. Further, helping children discover their escalation pattern will give them a chance to learn to manage and redirect their feelings and emotions before they become too overwhelming.

3. Once the child can identify his or her pattern of escalation, work with the child to make a plan for what

to do when he or she is overwhelmed – when life becomes too intense. This plan should include a way to relax and redirect his or her energy away from the emotional throngs of intensity.

4. Should the explosion happen anyway, it is important to remain calm and create a distance between your emotions and the child's. Anger and frustration always beget more anger and frustration, so it is really important for the adults working with the child to stay emotionally neutral.

5. Take a breather. This goes for the child and the adults. The best way to create the distance I talked about above is to remember to take a break and calm down.

6. Remember to focus on the good behavior you want to see. All too often, we get into a pattern of responding to the negative behaviors strongly (because these behaviors emotionally hook us) and not responding enough, to the positive behaviors. The result – more negative behaviors. So, do a mental inventory and make sure to focus your time and energy on the positive behaviors.

7. Behavioral outbursts, whether internal or external, are teachable moments. Yes, they are frustrating and annoying, maybe even infuriating. But they are still teachable moments. Take the time to redirect the behavior, focusing on teaching the GT child how to understand and redirect the behavior.

The bottom line to all of this: Intensity is not a bad thing in and of itself. Intensity is passion, the kind of passion we use to create. But the way in which the GT child copes with his or her intensity can be a problem. Utilizing some of the strategies above can go a long way to helping both kids and adults embrace the intensity and recognize it for what it is – a wonderful aspect of what it means to be gifted in the first place!

Christine Fonseca has worked in the field of education for more than a decade. Relying on her expertise as a school psychologist, behavioral consultant, speaker, and parenting expert, she has been a resource for parents and children in understanding the social and emotional needs of gifted children. She is the author of several books, including Emotional Intensity in Gifted Students *and* 101 Success Secrets for Gifted Kids. *You can learn more about Christine and her work at http://christinefonseca.com.*

Using Books to Meet the Social and Emotional Needs of Gifted Students

By Judith Wynn Halsted

As readers of this newsletter are acutely aware, even gifted children whose intellectual needs are adequately met have other needs, as well. The very existence of SENG is a response to the recognition that our gifted children often face social and emotional challenges that differ from those of their classmates. They need to understand and learn to cope with their differences—and ideally, they will learn to thrive because of them.

In broad outline, as they grow, gifted children must develop several skills:

- Recognize and accept that their level of intellectual or artistic ability is not shared by everyone—that they are, indeed, different;
- Understand that they may need more time alone than other children do (and be supported by adults who understand this, too);
- Learn to build relationships with other people, many of whom do not share their abilities and interests;
- Learn how to use their abilities well, even when doing

so sets them apart from many others; and

- Learn to take responsibility for finding ways to satisfy their intellectual curiosity and to express their creativity.

In addition, depending on each child's nature and personality, he or she may need to address more specific issues, such as creativity, intensity, introversion, a high level of moral concerns, perfectionism, and sensitivity, among others. This is a tall order, and gifted children and adolescents need the support of adults—parents as well as teachers—who understand, accept, and are able to help them meet the social and emotional challenges they face simply because they are gifted.

Parents who need background information will find helpful resources online, in organizations like SENG, and in the many books published in the last several years related to various aspects of growing up gifted. When they have acquired an understanding of the issues and are ready to step in with a practical approach to helping their child, these parents can turn to books again—this time, to children's books.

When an adult and child both read a book in which the characters deal with some of the same issues the child is facing, they are preparing for a meaningful discussion that might not happen otherwise. After all, the characters in books are separate from the child—it is often easier for a child to talk about the problems of a fictional character than about her own problems. Reading and then discussing books with children is an easy, readily available, inexpensive, and very pleasant way of helping children think and talk about the situations they face—a non-threatening approach, because they are talking about someone else.

This kind of discussion may take place in a school setting,

through a pull-out gifted program, or with a small group in a regular classroom. It requires three components: a teacher or librarian to make it happen, enough copies of a selected book for each child in the group, and time in the schedule for the group to meet–preferably with a modicum of privacy–for discussion. The program is similar to a Junior Great Books™ discussion group, but the books and the questions are chosen specifically for the gifted children who have been selected to join the group, with their social and emotional characteristics in mind.

Whether or not such a program is available at school, parents can offer a more personalized version of the same opportunity at home. Home schooling parents certainly can arrange to fit reading and discussing books into the curriculum. It is a natural way of communicating with children, especially for parents who love to read. And parents as well as teachers can organize boys' or girls' groups to talk about books.

The process involves selecting an appropriate book, reading the book and developing questions, introducing the book to the child, and after the child has read it, and enjoying an open-ended discussion.

Selecting appropriate books.

First, books chosen for discussion with gifted children should be well-written and intellectually challenging. The language should stretch their vocabulary and reflect the time or place in which the story is set, offering them a broader experience with language than they find in their daily lives. In some of their books, plots should be unresolved, causing readers to consider alternative possibilities and choices. Books for these readers should make good use of literary devices such as metaphor, flashbacks, and alternating narrators. Humor should be on a spontaneous, creative level.

In addition, books selected for discussion of social and emotional needs will have characters who are experiencing some of the same issues as the child who will read them: making friends, establishing an identity, feeling alone or different, standing up for a conviction, intensity, perfectionism, or other characteristics of gifted children and adults.

Of course, not everything a gifted child reads has to be this serious; escape reading is useful and valid when we recognize it for what it is and know when and why we are choosing it. But lightweight reading will not bear the weight of the kind of discussion we are proposing here.

Reading the book and developing questions.

Questions may occur as you are reading the book; jot these down to consider later. If you can assume that the child has read and understood the book, you can skip over fact questions and focus on thought questions: What does the child *think* about the book? Not what happened, but why did it happen, why did a character react as he or she did, what would the child have done in the same situation? How did a character *feel* in a given instance? Does the child know others who have felt or done the same thing? What is the child's response to this?

Before you begin a conversation with your child, you may want to write your questions down. A list of five to ten questions will be a good start for a 20-minute discussion; you probably will not get to all of them, but you will feel more confident if you begin with more than you need.

Introduce the book to the child.

Perhaps you and your child have selected the book together, or maybe you are working with a book your child introduced to you–in which case this step is not necessary. But if the book was your choice, you will want to explain why you chose the book, what you liked about it, and why you think your child will enjoy it–while stirring in a little mystery to arouse your child's curiosity. Perhaps there is a character in the book who reminds you of the child or of one of her friends, or a situation that reminds you of an experience your family has had. You may want to mention this, without explaining further, to whet the child's interest.

Enjoy an open-ended discussion.

Ask your first question and listen to your child's response. Your purpose is not to tell him what you think, but to learn what he thinks. Allow him the time to formulate an answer and articulate his opinion. There are no right or wrong answers, only the child's current answer–it may change upon further consideration. If this first question is fruitful, ask follow-up questions. It does not matter if you never get to your next question, as long as the discussion flows freely.

Much more specific and detailed information on this process is found in my book, *Some of My Best Friends Are Books,* cited below. To provide examples, here are abbreviated versions of a few annotations in the book's bibliography, with some of the suggested questions.

Early Elementary: Kindergarten to Grade 2
Hannah, by Gloria Whelan

Hannah is nine in 1887; she is blind, and has never gone to school. But when the new teacher, boarding at her house, asks if Hannah can go to school, her mother relents. The first day does not go well. Carl, the oldest boy in the one-room school, teases Hannah and trips her, and she gets lost trying to find her way home alone. The new Braille device that could help her learn to read costs five dollars—too much for her parents. Then comes the potato harvest, with a prize for the person who gathers the most potatoes. The contrite Carl, who has won the prize for the last two years, has an idea that surprises Hannah.

- *Differentness.* How is Hannah made to feel different from others? In what ways have you helped someone who is different feel comfortable in a group?
- *Relationships with others.* What are all the reasons you can think of that Hannah's mother does not want her to go to school? Do you know of someone who sounds gruffer than he or she actually is? What does Hannah do that helps people learn to like her?
- *Resilience.* How was Hannah able to keep herself so strong-minded and able to overcome obstacles?
- *Sensitivity.* What exactly happens at school that causes Hannah to try to go home alone? How could she have reacted differently?

Upper Elementary: Grades 3 – 5
Millicent Min, Girl Genius, by Lisa Yee

Millicent is 11 years old, will be a high school senior in the fall, and has talked her parents into allowing her to take a college course in poetry this summer. They have agreed that she will tutor Stanford Wong in English, with the hope that he can pass sixth grade and play basketball. Millie misunderstands him because she assumes that all gifted people are interested in academics. She also misunderstands her new friend Emily Ebers, neglecting to tell Emily about her outstanding academic record, and then slow to believe that when Emily learns about it she is upset not because Millicent is so smart, but because Millicent was not honest with Emily.

- *Aloneness; Introversion.* Sometimes Millie is lonely, and sometimes she enjoys being alone. What makes the difference between the two for her? For you?
- *Arrogance; Differentness.* Does Millicent's writing make her sound arrogant to you? Do you think she is arrogant?
- *Identity; Using ability.* What different kinds of giftedness are exemplified by the characters in this book? Millie knows most about intellectual giftedness— how does this contribute to her cluelessness? What can you learn from her?
- *Relationships with others.* Is it better, as Maddie says, to be liked than right? How do you decide to be liked or right in different situations?

Middle School: Grades 6 – 8
Fever, by Laurie Halse Anderson

In the hot, dry August of 1793, people in Philadelphia began dying of yellow fever. When Matilda's mother is stricken and Matilda and her grandfather decide to go to friends in the countryside, they find that the city has been quarantined. They both become ill, recover, and return to a nearly deserted and anarchic Philadelphia. Matilda survives by finding Eliza, the free black woman who had cooked for her parents' coffeehouse. Finally, in late October, the frost arrives and the fever abates. On November 10th, President Washington returns to the capital city. By then, Matilda is already picking up the pieces of her life. This thoroughly researched and fast-paced novel evokes the fear and horror of the disease, but also the courage and sacrifice of people who helped each other survive.

- *Drive to understand.* In the early years of our history as the United States, the Industrial Revolution had not yet reached America, and everyday life was much as it had been during the Colonial period. What changes would occur in Matilda's life by 1830 or 1840?
- *Moral concerns.* Was it right or wrong for the rich and powerful people to leave the poor and powerless behind in Philadelphia? Was it right or wrong for Matilda and Grandfather to leave her mother?

Senior High: Grades 9 – 12
The Gospel According to Larry, by Janet Tashjian

In a prologue, the author is approached in a grocery store parking lot by a young man who convinces her to read the manuscript that he hands to her. What follows is the manuscript—Josh Swensen's story of how his life changed after he built a website to protest consumerism. Josh is bright and thoughtful, a critical thinker with a sense of humor and a serious goal: to make a contribution, to change the world. But the website takes on a life its own; the media frenzy tears Josh's world apart and he must re-evaluate his goals.

- *Differentness; Identity.* What strengths in Josh's character help him to go forward after the media learn that he created the website? In what ways is his differentness his strength? How is he able to be so comfortable with it?
- *Intensity.* If you are as intense about your interests as Josh is, you may find it useful to think about his comment that he has been "caring more about my message than about the people in my life." Do you agree

with Josh's conclusion? Are there situations when interests might reasonably take precedence over people? What interests cause you to experience intensity, and how do you balance your interests with people?

Resources: Books

Halsted, Judith Wynn. *Some of My Best Friends Are Books: Guiding Gifted Readers,* 3rd ed.m 2009. Great Potential Press. http://www.giftedbooks.com

Hauser, Paula & Gail A. Nelson. *Books for the Gifted Child* (Vol. 2). 1988. Bowker.

Resources: Websites

Children's Literature Web Guide: www.ucalgary.ca/~dkbrown

Hoagies Gifted Information Page:
http://www.hoagiesgifted.com

Outstanding Books for the College Bound:
http://www.ala.org/yalsa/booklists/obcb

Judith Wynn Halsted has retired from a long career in education. She completed a Master's degree in Library Science at the University of Illinois, and was the librarian at The Pathfinder School. In 1988 she published the first edition of Guiding Gifted Readers, *Updated editions of her book, titled* Some of My Best Friends Are Books, *were published in 1994, 2002, and 2009.*

Encouraging Emotional Intelligence

By Steven I. Pfeiffer

We know that in the U.S. today, the prevalence of mental health problems among children and youth — including those who are gifted — is alarmingly high. Some authorities estimate as many as one in five students has significant psychological problems such as depression, anxiety, low self-esteem, eating disorders and social maladjustment. Although growing up has never been easy, today's youth face new and more challenging social pressures. Gifted children are not impervious to developing psychological problems. And, in some instances, what makes gifted children special paradoxically can serve to increase their risk for social and emotional difficulties.

I've written elsewhere on parenting principles that can help serve to protect a gifted child from developing psychological problems. At the 2006 NAGC conference in Charlotte, N.C., I spoke about how these very principles promote healthy psychological development among gifted children and youth. I would like to take this opportunity to introduce SENG readers to one of the principles, encouraging social intelligence. I will include a brief description of a gifted child who I worked with in my clinical practice to help illustrate the relevance of the principle.

Encouraging social intelligence ensures that your gifted child develops the important skills to be courteous, a good listener, likable, helpful, trustworthy, a team player, able to get along with others, and empathic. These important social skills have been variously labeled in the professional literature as emotional intelligence, social competence, social maturity, and interpersonal intelligence. In my clinical practice, I like to consider these skills part of social intelligence. These skills do not automatically develop. In working with gifted children and their parents in my consulting office and during my tenure as director of Duke University's summer gifted program, I have encountered many extraordinarily gifted and talented children with extraordinarily underdeveloped social intelligence. Guiding your gifted child to develop social intelligence will increase the likelihood that your son or daughter will enjoy a rich, meaningful, and successful life.

Gifted children with well-developed social intelligence are at ease with peers and adults, self-confident, able to rein in emotional impulse and master stress, and accurately read social cues and tolerate frustrating situations. They present themselves as friendly and appealing, almost as if they have taken a Dale Carnegie course in "How to Make Friends and Influence People!"

Margot (this child's name has been disguised to protect her anonymity) was an intellectually gifted 7-year old who was quickly developing a bad reputation in her private school as a troubled student. At the headmaster's encouragement, I was invited by her parents to observe Margot in her classroom. I quickly observed that her problems represented underdeveloped social intelligence. Margot was reluctant to share with others or respect her classmates' property, would not wait her turn, was uncooperative in group activities, and demonstrated little respect for teacher authority.

Rather than viewing Margot as a troubled child with deep-seated emotional problems (or conversely, as a misunderstood gifted child), her parents and I embarked upon a course of treatment that focused on teaching Margot important social skills. In less than three months, combining individual, family and parent counseling sessions, we identified friendship-making problems and how to correct them, instructed Margot in social etiquette and good sportsmanship, and provided Margot with a vocabulary of emotional words to help her better identify the feelings of others. Outside of sessions, I assigned Margot's parents literature and popular movies to further reinforce social skills and deepen our work in building social intelligence. For example, while watching a movie at home with her parents, Margot was asked to identify good and bad social behavior among the various actors.

Margot and other gifted children do not come into the world knowing these important skills. Even highly gifted children need to learn from their parents about virtuous habits, good manners, and how to get along with others. This is an important component of what we consider character development. The ingredients for teaching social intelligence include the following:

- Set a good example. There is nothing more powerful than teaching by quiet example.
- Make standards clear and expectations high, but not unreasonable.
- Talk about right and wrong. Don't preach but rather hold Socratic dialogues with your gifted child.
- Avoid rescuing your child. Although it is tempting to want to solve your child's problems, it robs your son or

daughter of the opportunity to develop problem-solving skills, confidence and self-sufficiency.

- Look for warning signs. The following behaviors may suggest that you need to give greater attention to your child's social intelligence: acts like a poor loser, lacks confidence, plays too aggressively, doesn't have a friend, upsets easily or quickly becomes angry, acts bossy, doesn't share or respect others' property, is uncooperative, doesn't do well in group situations, doesn't respect authority, rarely compromises, shows little or no empathy for others' feelings, acts discourteously. If you think that your gifted child is exhibiting one or more of these warning signs to a degree that is excessive, unreasonable, and/or adversely impacting upon their school, family or social life, consider seeking a professional consultation.

Conclusion

Although the great majority of gifted children enjoy better-than-average social adjustment, some of them do experience stressful psychological problems. As a parent, you have the responsibility and opportunity to teach your gifted son or daughter a myriad of social skills to help him or her more successfully navigate the often turbulent social and emotional waters of childhood and adolescence. Encouraging social intelligence is one important parenting principle that provides your child with an important set of social skills that increases the likelihood that he or she will enjoy a rich, meaningful, and successful life.

Steven Pfeiffer is a Professor at Florida State University, where he serves as Director of Clinical Training. Professor Pfeiffer is lead author of the Gifted Rating Scales, and coauthor of the Devereux Behavior Rating Scales. He recently authored a book for practitioners, Serving the Gifted: Evidence-Based Clinical and Psycho-educational Practice *(Routledge, 2012) and served as Guest Editor for a special issue on giftedness for the* Journal of Psychoeducational Assessment *(Volume 30, Number 1, February 2012).*

Parenting Twice-exceptional Children

By Dina Brulles

Nothing has ever been easy with David. Nothing. Ever. David is a nice kid. He is smart and quiet. He blends in well enough that not many people, including teachers, notice the learning difficulties he has. He does not usually draw attention to himself; he does not get into trouble; he gets by OK. David, who is highly gifted, also has been diagnosed with severe Attention Deficit Disorder (ADD – no "H"), is highly gifted, has an Obsessive Compulsive Disorder (OCD – Tricotillamania), and a learning disability (LD – dysgraphia and dyslexia).

Like many parents of twice-exceptional children, I always knew that David was different from other children. The differences were not subtle ones. As an infant, he began screaming before opening his eyes upon awakening. As a toddler and through adolescence, he would routinely and calmly break into a cold sweat and faint for reasons caused by stress, but not apparent to others. At nearly eighteen, he is still not driving because he forgets to practice so that he can take the driving test. It is better this way.

Transitions have always been very difficult for David. A painful reminder occurs with the evolution of every new day – the most consistent, but physically and mentally drastic

93

transition we face. Bright lights, loud sounds and other external stimuli barely noticeable to others cause David physical and emotional pain. The obvious solution is to stay away from situations where these may transpire. However, staying away from people and life is not only not an option, but is unhealthy. Although his social interactions have been limited to a few individuals, I have noticed that David responds well to those few people. Perhaps it is because those few people have been a constant throughout his life; perhaps because of the empathy or acceptance he feels from those few individuals; perhaps because those feelings of acceptance are so rare, they mean more.

Children like David, with extreme sensitivities, are unusual. Because of the sometimes-intense reactions that they may display, they are commonly seen as sources of their own supposed digressions from 'normal behavior.' But these behaviors are normal for them. How does one inform and convince another that what he perceives to be normal is not? All of this can be understood and accepted by parents of these uniquely gifted children. Yet, to teachers and other adults, we still find ourselves defending them, saying, "No one would choose to impose this upon herself." Neither the behaviors nor the diagnoses are choices. They are real, and are generally physiologically based. We need to help teach the children how to develop coping and managing strategies so they can build on their strengths and pursue their talents. And we need to help others understand this need.

The Davids of the world commonly follow similar paths. If the youth has no support system – a close family member or mentor – who seeks out assistance and resources, the child may likely drop out of school, whether in high school or in college. On the other hand, the twice-exceptional child who has an active advocate can develop his or her strengths like other gifted individuals. It takes perseverance.

The journey is as challenging as can be the child's behaviors: it is trying and can be exhausting for parents. Parents fight a lifetime of emotions in any given day. Over time, and to some degree, parents may experience desperation, feel a strong need to protect their child, feel self-doubt, and self-blame. But we always have hope and love. With some effort and some luck, we find support and acceptance from others who care for, educate, and counsel uniquely gifted children.

We learn to accept, because we know that despite what others may be believe, we have committed ourselves to guiding these misunderstood individuals. We accept that the challenges the child faces will continue, and for this reason, we must continue with our efforts even when it reaches beyond our own children. We must continue to seek advice when needed, and must continue to educate others: parents, teachers, school administrators, school counselors, and other caring professionals who work with children.

We must also understand our role. We cannot blame others for not understanding. Unless you have lived with and loved a child with dual-exceptionalities, you cannot have the full picture. It is our role to help educate others, to be the gentle reminder that not all gifted children have the ability to pursue their strengths and talents to the same degree, and to provide information that will guide others.

Because David is smart, he generally gets by in school. However, with each year in school, getting by has become increasingly, and understandably, more difficult. Elementary school teachers receive pre-service training in child development, special education, and other coursework that helps them to understand how children learn. Armed with this training, most elementary education teachers naturally create nurturing environments that are accepting of differences. A shift in teachers' mind-sets occurs in the transition through the middle school to high school years. We typically find that middle school teachers begin to make fewer accommodations for diverse learners. Middle school teachers come to expect certain behaviors from adolescents seized by hormones. Some may assume that all the students' behaviors are based upon choices students are intentionally making. This attitude results in the teachers' decreased effort to recognize the source of the behaviors being portrayed in the classroom, and to then seek ways to work with the child. It was at this grade level that I obtained a Section 504 Accommodation Plan for my son. I realized that he would need it going into high school.

I was both right and wrong. David did need the plan, and ideally, it would serve him well. A Section 504 Accommodation Plan* is a legally binding document that spells out the specific accommodations teachers need to make as determined by the disabling factor(s) the child experiences based on a specific diagnosis. 504 Plans are not given lightly. The parent or guardian must show that the disabling factor(s) prevent the student from learning in the classroom without modifications and/or accommodations made to the curriculum and instruction. I was wrong in believing that the plan would be the answer to the instructional modifications David needed. It was an attempt made so that David could survive in the accelerated and Advanced Placement classes he qualified to take.

High school teachers are content area specialists. Their training is in their domain – English, History, Chemistry, etc. Therein lies the problem for twice-exceptional students. The teachers oftentimes do not know that twice-exceptional students might not learn the content in the same way others students learn. High school teachers may see one to two hundred students a day. It is very difficult to keep track of the special learning needs of students in a large high school setting. The teachers have learned that they must treat students "equally," so that they are "fair" and "consistent" in their expectations and grading. (Ouch.) However, we cannot blame the teachers; this is what they know; this is what is supported by their school administration. Schools are created in a very linear sequential way; twice-exceptional children are not. The traditional high school may not be the best fit for the twice-exceptional child. For those students and parents who select this model, there will most likely be challenges.

Our children did not seek out the exceptionalities they have. We know that no one would choose the pain and confusion that a twice-exceptional person endures. I have spent decades seeking answers to unanswerable questions. My efforts to guide others have directed my own life. As I have struggled along this journey, I have found explanations and understanding. I found relief in the recognition that I am not alone. For those of you struggling along this journey with me, I invite you to join the SENG community. At SENG's summer gifted conferences, parents, children, educators and mental health professionals interact and learn with others who share similar concerns. You may also wish to support SENG's mission by offering financial donations to this non-profit organization. I encourage you to explore the SENG website to discover the myriad of ways you can join others who seek to support the emotional needs of the gifted.

Recommended reading

Learning Outside the Lines, by Jonathon Mooney
Uniquely Gifted, edited by Kiesa Kay
The Visual-Spatial Learner, by Linda Silverman
Guiding the Gifted Child, by James T. Webb, Elizabeth
    Meckstroth, and Stephanie Tolan
Misdiagnosis and Dual Diagnoses of Gifted Children and
    Adults, by Webb, Amend, Webb, Goerss, Beljan, & Olenchak

*A student eligible for Section 504 is defined as follows: "An individual who has a physical or mental impairment that substantially limits a major life activity, has a record of such impairment or is regarded as having such an impairment. The law sets no list of specific diseases and conditions that constitute physical or mental impairments forth. The criteria are tied to whether the disability substantially limits a major life activity, such as learning."

Dina Brulles is the Director of Gifted Education in the Paradise Valley Unified School District, Arizona, and faculty member of Arizona State University where she teaches gifted education. Dina is Past President of the Arizona Association for Gifted and Talented, past SENG Board Director, and a gifted education consultant. Publications include The Cluster Grouping Handbook, *Free Spirit Publishing, and* Helping All Gifted Children Learn, *published by Pearson Assessment.*

September Back-To-School Suggestions

By Wenda Sheard

SENG's vision is a world where gifted, talented, and creative individuals are supported to build gratifying, meaningful lives and contribute to the well-being of others.

How can parents best support their gifted, talented, and creative children at the beginning of the school year? I offer three suggestions.

Teach Children Philosophies of Education

I suggest that parents discuss with their children the purpose of education. Exposing young children to what great philosophers have thought about education not only teaches children history, philosophy, and education, but also helps them to create their own educational goals—goals that may differ significantly from the goals of other children.

When exploring what great philosophers have thought about education, children might notice three main purposes of education:

1. Education serves the purpose of preparing children for adult life, including preparing them to support

themselves as adults. Accordingly, the United States Department of Education's stated mission is: "to promote student achievement and preparation for global competitiveness by fostering educational excellence and ensuring equal access."

2. Some philosophers emphasize that education should prepare children for good citizenship. Plato (circa 400 B.C.) and John Locke (1632-1704) advocated virtue and good citizenship as the aims of education. Plato wrote: "And we must remember further that we are speaking of the education, not of a trainer, or of the captain of a ship, but of a perfect citizen who knows how to rule and how to obey." Locke wrote: "Learning must be had, but in the second place, as subservient only to greater qualities."

3. Education also serves the purpose of providing children with an enjoyable childhood worth living and remembering fondly. John Dewey (1859-1952) felt strongly that education should respect childhood: "[The best teachers] give the pupils something to do, not something to learn; and the doing is of such a nature as to demand thinking or the intentional noting of connections; learning naturally results." Maria Montessori (1870-1952) similarly advocated happy childhoods: "Education is not something which the teacher does ... it is a natural process which develops spontaneously in the human being."

Once children understand the purposes of education, they have tools to articulate whether, and how, their own educations meet those purposes or might be tweaked to meet those purposes. Sometimes the only tweaking necessary is a change of perspective—perhaps a child will understand that even if school currently is not sufficiently rigorous in the "heading to adult life" sense. Perhaps the child can find ways to enjoy childhood until rigor appears or reappears. Or, better yet, perhaps the child can find ways to introduce rigor into his or her own education. Child-introduced rigor might include education that will lead to employment and/or good citizenship in future years. Some children spend time excelling in computer programming, gaining marketable skills at a young age. Other children spend time volunteering in ways that make a difference in the world, foster virtue in the child, and later impress college admissions officers and employers.

Explain the Necessity of Knowledge, Communion, and Expression

Another way that parents might support their gifted, talented, and creative children at the beginning of the school year is by reading P. Susan Jackson's article "Bright Star – Black Sky: A Phenomenological Study of Depression as a Window into the Psyche of the Gifted Adolescent (see the end of this column for the online link). I recommend that parents read the article first before deciding whether, when, and how to share the article's excellent insights with their children.

In the article, Jackson explains that gifted teens have an absolute need for knowledge of themselves and of physical and spiritual phenomena, for strong emotional or spiritual communion with others, and for expression of their emotions and feelings. Reading the article at the beginning of each school year might help parents and children (if sufficiently mature) to understand that beginning a school year is not a simple matter; each school year presents new opportunities and challenges for finding the knowledge, communion, and expression that Jackson found critical to the lives of gifted teens.

During the first weeks of the school year, parents and children can consider how the school year will affect all aspects of each child's life. Will the child have sufficient opportunities for knowledge and for self-knowledge? Will the child have time at school or elsewhere to interact with true peers, not just age-mates? Will the child have time and methods to express emotions and feelings? Parents and children should consider finding non-school times to fill whatever gaps might exist in a given child's school hours.

Offer Social and Emotional Hints

Most parents understand that the acquisition of knowledge is a small part of any school experience. Most teachers are keenly aware that the school day involves not just knowledge, but also social times and emotional events. In this last section, I offer three hints that parents might offer their gifted, talented, and creative children at the beginning of a new school year.

The first hint comes from Benjamin Franklin, who realized that by asking someone a favor, you endear yourself to that person. Counterintuitive, yes, but it works! I suggest that you and your child research what's known as the Benjamin Franklin Effect. Your child might then decide to try out Franklin's idea at school as a way to build friendship and respect.

Another friendship-building hint that I have shared over the years with new students is to look around the room and find students who look lonely. Then, with a smile on your face, go up to each of those children, ask them about themselves, and listen well. Smiling is a fantastic way to gain friends. Helping others who look lonely is an excellent way to exhibit and to build a generous spirit. Asking people about themselves and listening carefully to their answers is a social skill that even many adults could improve.

Sometimes a gifted, talented, and creative child will spend a school year without true peers in school. When this happens, parents can share yet another hint—encourage the child to approach the school year with the lens of an anthropologist.

Yes, that's right—teach the child about the field of anthropology and engage the child in studying the culture of the school. Learning about anthropology and applying an anthropological lens, at the child's level of understanding, to the school experience will help the gifted child learn about and reflect a great deal on people, social structures, and child development. Parents who spend the time necessary to guide their budding anthropologist will benefit from increased and honest communication that might lead to better understanding of the child's school experience.

Conclusion

For more hints and suggestions, I recommend the book A Parent's Guide to Gifted Children (Great Potential Press, 2007). That book, which is the core of the SENG Model Parenting Groups, well explains the nature and nurture of gifted, talented, and creative children.

If there is a SENG Model Parenting Group starting in your area, I highly recommend that you join the group. If no groups are currently available in your area, I recommend you consider being trained as a SENG Model Parent Group facilitator. For more information, visit http://www.sengifted.org.

References

Jackson, P. Susan, "Bright star — black sky: A phenomenological study of depression as a window into the psyche of the gifted adolescent," Roeper Review. 1998 Feb 20(3) 215-221, available online at http://www.sengifted.org/resources/resource-library/articles-library.

Wenda Sheard is an attorney, teacher, and mother of three gifted children. After practicing law for nearly twenty years, she earned a Ph.D. in political science with an emphasis on education policy. From 2004-2006, Dr. Sheard lived in Hangzhou, China and taught at an international school. She's currently living outside London, England and teaching at an international school.

Gifted Education:

What I Wished I Had Known Sooner!

By Carolyn Kottmeyer

I started learning about gifted education by accident of birth: my first daughter's birth. As with most things she's taught me, I had no idea I was learning at first. Over the years, I've learned a great deal about gifted education; and there are a few things that I wished I'd learned much earlier...

1. Giftedness comes in different levels.

Not all gifted kids are the same. My first learning experience in education was with our elementary school principal, as my daughter was enrolled for first grade. The principal explained that "Gifted is like a light switch – it's either on or off." I can't put it any other way: she was wrong.

Some children are moderately gifted, and need a little more depth and breadth than the regular curriculum offers. These are the kids who usually thrive in the typical gifted pull-out program, spending a few hours a week with their same-age gifted peers doing fun extension work.

Other gifted kids are more than "just plain gifted." These children used to be identified as highly, exceptionally, or profoundly gifted; but the latest versions of IQ tests aren't designed to differentiate levels of giftedness. The high ability of these kids may be obvious – reading *Charlotte's Web* in Kindergarten with understanding and delight, or doing algebra in elementary school. It may also be less obvious. These kids might sit quietly, never learning in the "age-grade" classroom, but not making a fuss about it. Or worse, they may *not* sit quietly, making a fuss, and becoming a discipline or behavior problem without anyone noticing their gifts. These more highly gifted children are far rarer than moderately gifted children, and a teacher may never encounter one in 30 years of teaching. Even among the most highly gifted children, there are differences. One child might be a prodigious writer or artist; another might excel in mathematics, mastering calculus before he enters puberty; while a third might prefer to learn all she can about the sciences and search for the cure for cancer. Gifted children may not find a social fit among their age-peers, and not all gifted children will get along with each other. It's important that we allow them to spend time among their academic peers, and help them to find those true friends they seek.

Along with different levels of giftedness, there are different educational options for gifted children. *A Nation Deceived* (http://www.nationdeceived.org/), a report detailing years of research, shows that our gifted children need an appropriate education, and that there are many different ways to provide the accelerated education that can meet their needs.

2. Most teachers and administrators are not experts in gifted education.

It's not their fault, but it's true. Most teachers and administrators (as well as counselors, psychologists, and doctors) have no formal education in giftedness. If they're lucky, in four years of pre-service education there might have been a single chapter in a special education course that mentioned gifted children. More likely, according to an informal survey by Jim Delisle, Professor of Education at Kent State University in Ohio, teachers' pre-service education in the U.S. didn't include even a mention of gifted children.

What does this mean for teachers who encounter a gifted or exceptionally gifted child? It means they must do their own research and reading to learn how to serve the child appropriately. Thanks to the Internet, that's not as hard as it sounds. There are support groups for teachers of the gifted, and plenty of research and resources on gifted education. The Internet even offers professional development programs for teachers.

What does this mean for parents who encounter a teacher who just "doesn't get" their gifted child? It means that we parents have the opportunity to work together with the teacher to both grow and learn along the way – keeping in mind that it's a fine line to walk between "helpful partner" and "pushy parent." It's a path we can, and must, learn to walk, with practice and with help from the Internet. There we can find support groups for parents of the gifted as well as research and other resources.

3. Gifted children can also be learning disabled.

Many people assume that gifted and learning disabled are opposite ends of the same scale. Teachers may assume that a child, identified as gifted but struggling in school, is simply lazy or unmotivated. At the same time, they may assume that a child identified as learning disabled cannot possibly be gifted. I wish I'd known sooner that neither of these assumptions is true. A child can be both gifted *and* learning disabled, a combination also known as "dually identified," "twice exceptional," or "2e."

Some estimates put the number of gifted and learning disabled children at up to 10 percent of all gifted children, similar to the percentage of learning disabled children in the general population. Once a child is identified with a single learning disability (LD), the odds that she has additional LDs are much greater.

Imagine being a gifted child with amazing strengths in some areas, while at the same time struggling with basic learning skills that everyone assumes should come easily to a bright child. It can't be easy to live in that body. To some parents' surprise, they discover, as they investigate their child's dual exceptionality, that they too were gifted/LD children.

Common disabilities that effect learning among gifted children include Asperger Syndrome and AD/HD. Gifted children can also have disabilities affecting visual or auditory processing, dyslexia affecting their reading and spelling skills, sensory processing disorder, and nonverbal learning disorder, among other LDs.

Disabilities are often overlooked at first because of gifted children's ability to compensate for their own weaknesses. Many gifted dyslexics aren't discovered until third or fourth grade, when the reading requirements of school surpass the child's ability to memorize and work around reading difficulties. AD/HD and other executive function disabilities might not show up until middle or high school, when the organizational demands of school surpass the gifted child's ability to hide her difficulties.

Conversely, if the disability is severe enough to be noticed in the lower grades, it's the child's giftedness that might be overlooked. The fact that a child with AD/HD cannot sit still will be noticed long before his ability to learn much higher-level material may be discovered. The gifted and Asperger's child may look out of place socially from the earliest grades, overshadowing his advanced academic abilities.

4. Gifted education doesn't have to be elitist or expensive.

In our egalitarian society, we want all children to have an equal opportunity to a good education, but that doesn't mean that all kids learn at the same pace and at the same academic level. Many people believe that identifying certain children as gifted is a bad thing, that it creates a class structure between the "haves" and the "have-nots." Further, they feel that if the gifted education program is something that all children can benefit from, but is offered only to those identified as gifted, then the program is, indeed, elitist.

Gifted children come from all income levels, and all ethnic backgrounds. If we believe that gifted education divides children along socio-economic boundaries, then we're doing gifted identification wrong.

Many of our gifted children today find themselves in public schools stretched to the breaking point, especially in the time of No Child Left Behind. How can these schools ethically allocate money to the education of gifted children, who are already able to pass the annual high-stakes achievement tests? When we ask this, we are asking the wrong question. Instead, we should ask: How can we ethically ignore the appropriate education of an entire subset of the student population, the gifted children? Gifted education that consists of museum visits, robotic equipment, puzzles, and games is not truly gifted education. It may entertain the gifted kids to the point where the promise of the "fun" gifted program for a few hours each week can get them to sit quietly the rest of the week. But that "fun" enrichment program isn't necessarily appropriate. It's not meeting the educational needs of most gifted children. They need to learn at their own level, and their own pace and depth, just like all other children.

This can happen in the regular classroom. Some subjects lend themselves to more in-depth study; and many kids, not just the gifted child, would benefit from greater depth and enrichment. Social studies is an example. With this subject it's likely that a few kids, including the gifted child, would love to do their own research and present their findings to the class.

Other subjects don't lend themselves as easily to enrichment, like spelling. Once a child has mastered spelling of most three letter words, it's time to advance. Adding c-a-t, r-a-t, and b-a-t when the child can already spell d-i-f-f-i-c-u-l-t and t-a-s-k doesn't help – it's time to accelerate the curriculum. Basic arithmetic, too, is difficult to enrich. Once a child can add numbers without carrying, it's time to learn about carrying. Once she can multiply 3-digit numbers, it's time to move forward – learning to multiply 4-digit and 5-digit numbers is a trivial enrichment.

While there are classes elsewhere in the building at the gifted child's current education level, there is always a no-cost option for that child. It might take a little coordination on the part of the teachers, but isn't a child's education worth a little scheduling effort? Once a child passes the level of courses in her school or district, there are free or nearly free distance education options available, with just a little teacher supervision.

These are four things I wish I understood back when I first journeyed into gifted education. I share them with you in the hopes that you do not have to reinvent the journey that has taken me 10 years to travel!

Resources from Carolyn

Here are some recommendations on the Hoagies' Gifted Education Page and elsewhere:

Professional development courses in giftedness: http://www.hoagiesgifted.org/professional_development.htm

On-line support groups that focus on gifted and twice exceptional for teachers, parents, and kids: http://www.hoagiesgifted.org/on-line_support.htm

An introduction to twice-exceptional children for parents and educators: The *Spotlight on 2e* series of booklets: http://www.2enewsletter.com.

A guide to enriching the gifted child's education in the classroom: *Teaching Gifted Kids in the Regular Classroom: Strategies and Techniques Every Teacher Can Use to Meet the Academic Needs of the Gifted and Talented*, by Susan Winebrenner

Free full curriculum units for grades K-12: http://www.hoagiesgifted.org/investigations.htm

Free high school and college-level curriculum options in all subjects: http://www.hoagiesgifted.org/online_hs.htm%20

SENG Director Carolyn Kottmeyer is the founder and director of Hoagies' Gifted Education Page and Hoagies' Kids and Teens Page. She has bachelor's and master's degrees in software engineering and developed an interest in gifted education a few years after the birth of her first child, when she noticed how the 'normal' path through education didn't seem to fit her. Since 1998, she has written for gifted newsletters and journals around the world.

Finding the Glory — On and Off
the Playing Field

By Linda C. Neumann

On the school athletic field, it seems that everyone expects and reveres top-level performance. A common expectation is that schools will offer special programs and opportunities to help athletes develop and hone their abilities in competition. Equally common is allocating money in the education budget to athletic programs, facilities, and equipment.

"The athletically gifted, in our society and in almost all cultures across the globe, are highly respected, looked up to, and even admired for their athletic gifts," says SENG board member Steven Pfeiffer, a psychologist and professor at Florida State University. "This special status comes early, to some as early as the elementary grades. The intellectually or academically gifted child, on the other hand, quite often is teased, taunted, disparaged, and treated with anything other than admiration, particularly in elementary and middle school."

Pfeiffer observed what he considers to be this striking difference in treatment between athletically and intellectually gifted students when he served as a sport psychologist for the women's soccer program at Duke University. This experience provided him with a unique opportunity to learn more about the lives of elite, young, female athletes. According to Pfeiffer, he discovered similarities as well as differences between the two groups of gifted students.

One of the most important similarities he found is that all children fortunate enough to have a gift – athletic, academic, or artistic – require the same basics to reach their potential: good teachers, hard work over an extended period of time, and often a mentor to guide them. He observes, "No matter what the gift, natural ability alone rarely, if ever, leads to full actualization of one's talent. This lesson is often a difficult one for both the highly gifted athlete and the highly gifted student to accept! Whether it's long hours spent on the playing field and in the weight room or it's long hours spent in the physics lab, one needs to put in the time and commit to sweat and hard work to accomplish big goals!"

The disparity in attitudes toward the athletically gifted and the academically gifted can be hard for both students and parents to take. Pfeiffer states, "I spend a lot of time talking about this difference with gifted youngsters that I treat in my private practice." With parents, who may feel that their academically gifted student is being short changed, Pfeiffer works to change their focus from the short term to the long term.

In the here-and-now, parents of academically gifted children are often focused on how to provide their own gifted son or daughter with a more challenging and intellectually stimulating classroom experience. "This makes a lot of sense," explains Pfeiffer, "but if the parent pushes too hard or in a way that antagonizes others, the outcome may not be beneficial for the gifted child."

To avoid this situation, Pfeiffer asks parents to think about how they would like others to describe their son or daughter in the future – to focus on the long-range goals, wishes, expectations, and fears the parents have for their gifted child. With this shift in focus, according to Pfeiffer, "parental concerns quickly take on a new, different, and, I would argue, very important slant – a slant well-worth discussing." The discussion of long-range and short-term goals becomes even more interesting and productive when teachers and gifted students join in. It can help all parties re-frame their view of a child, and it can help parents and teachers formulate a new set of long-range goals to consider as they address immediate, unmet academic needs.

Partnerships such as those that Pfeiffer's discussions help forge between parents and educators can help minimize the differences between the treatment that athletically gifted and the academically gifted students receive. But what about the glory? What can academically gifted students do that will bring them the rewards and recognition that those who excel athletically often receive? The answer is competition, and there are plenty of competitions open to those who excel in areas such as mathematics, science, geography, writing, and the arts. To start your search for competitions like these, check the resources below. Academic competition might lead not only to glory, but to scholarships as well!

Websites

The Educator's Reference Desk: http://www.eduref.org/
Imagine magazine's links to academic competitions:
   http://cty.jhu.edu/imagine/linkb.htm
Hoagies Gifted Education Page – Contests and Awards:
   http://www.hoagiesgifted.org/contests.htm

Books

Karnes, F.A., & Riley, T.L. (2005). Competitions for talented kids. Waco, TX: Prufrock Press.

Tallent-Runnels, M.T., & Candler-Lotven, A.C. (2007). Academic competitions for gifted students: A resource book for teachers and parents. Thousand Oaks, CA: Corwin Press.

Olszewski-Kubilius, P., Limburg-Weber, L., & Pfeiffer, S.I. (Eds.). (2003). Early gifts: Recognizing and nurturing children's talents. Waco, TX: Prufrock Press.

Pfeiffer, S.I. (Ed.). (2008). Handbook of giftedness in children. NY: Springer Publishing.

Linda C. Neumann is the editor of 2e: Twice-Exceptional Newsletter *(http://www.2eNewsletter.com), a bi-monthly publication aimed at parents, educators, advocates, and others who help twice-exceptional children reach their potential. A former SENG Director, she is also the author of the* Spotlight on 2e Series *of booklets that explore the combination of giftedness and learning challenges in children.*

Helping Your Gifted Child Through Divorce Part 1

By Lori Comallie-Caplan

Week Ten of the SENG Model Parent Group (SMPG) is a discussion around Chapter 11 of *A Parent's Guide to Gifted Children,* "Complexities of Successful Parenting." There are many complex topics in this discussion, but one of the most important is divorce and its impact on gifted children. Many SENG Model Parent Groups are eight-week groups and leave out this very important topic. As I see gifted children in my private practice, it has become very apparent that this topic needs to be addressed.

James Webb, Ph.D. writes in *A Parent's Guide to Gifted Children,* 'The consequences of divorce and family separation may be even more severe for gifted children because of their sensitivity to emotions." (p. 235)

Divorce can have many effects on the gifted and emotionally sensitive child. Children can develop insecurities and fears for the future. Many changes happen through the process of a divorce – changes in parenting styles, living arrangements, even schools and access to their friends. Questions arise, such as "Will we have to find a new place to live? Will I be able to keep my dog? Will I ever see my friends?" One parent is no longer in the home. Children may fear abandonment by the absent parent and also wonder if the parent at home will also leave them. If abandonment is not the issue, rejection may be. Many children feel rejected and unloved by the absent parent. Those feelings of abandonment and rejection can lead to thoughts of blame. Children may feel that the divorce was their fault, and feelings of fault can lead to shame and guilt. When children feel at fault for the divorce, they want to take responsibility for fixing things. When the parents do not reunite, the child may feel powerless. Additional feelings that children face during the process of a divorce include grief, depression, stress, anxiety, loneliness, and anger. How you approach the divorce process can help alleviate some of these stressors for the child. Even if your children are aware of the disintegration of your relationship, and they are not surprised by the divorce announcement, it is vital to focus on your children's feelings and put aside your own feelings when telling your children of the divorce. Remember that gifted children are very insightful, overexcitable, and complex thinkers and may ask some very difficult questions. When making the announcement, try to find some time when both parents can be present, when everyone is calm, and there is enough time to address all of the children's questions.

Remember the effects of divorce and match your explanation to those effects. Remember that children are probably worried about the future, so explain what will happen, and focus on how it will affect the children's lives. Explain who will live where, when the move will happen, and when the children will be able to see each parent.

Remember that the children may be thinking that they are to blame, so take time to reassure them that the divorce is not their fault and that both parents will continue to love and parent them. Allow the children time to ask questions and try to answer them as truthfully and factually as possible without blame or angry comments. Try to explain some of the feelings that they may have and that those feelings are normal in this situation. Let them know you will be willing to listen to them now or anytime in the future. Let them know that it is ok if they don't want to talk to you, but would rather talk with a trusted friend, another family member or even a counselor.

In part two of this article, I will explore how to help gifted children through the transition without falling into enmeshment or treating them as though they were adults.

SENG President Lori Comallie-Caplan is currently in private practice specializing in therapy and evaluation of gifted children and adolescents in Las Cruces, New Mexico. Mrs. Comallie-Caplan is a Certified Educational Diagnostician and Certified Frasier Talent Assessment Profile Evaluator. She also is a certified SENG (Supporting Emotional Needs of the Gifted) Model Parent Group Facilitator as well as a SENG Model Parent Group Facilitator Trainer. She frequently presents at SENG and NAGC annual conferences.

Helping Your Gifted Child Through Divorce
Part 2

By Lori Comallie-Caplan and Marc Caplan

O ver the last 27 years, I have had the opportunity to serve families and children pre- and post- divorce in a variety of roles, including educator, counselor, and mediator. Over the last 30 years, my husband, a clinical psychologist, has served children and families and the courts in a variety of roles: therapist, court-appointed custody evaluator and parenting coordinator. This article is a collaboration between the two of us.

Adultizing and Enmeshment

In "Helping Your Gifted Child through Divorce, Part 1," we ended with being careful about falling into the traps of adultizing and enmeshment. Adultizing is talking to and leaning on a child for advice and emotional support. It is easier to fall into the trap of adultizing the gifted child than the typically developing child because sometimes gifted children seem more like adults than children in their vocabulary and ability to converse on an adult level. For this reason, it can be all too easy for a parent to share things that are inappropriate for a child to hear. In one family that I have worked with, the mother had an affair and told her teenage son to assuage her guilt and because she had "no one" else to talk to. The affair may have happened because her husband and she had drifted apart and she had no support system of friends. That still doesn't make it appropriate to share that type of information with the gifted child.

In the SENG Model Parenting Group Book, *A Parent's Guide to the Gifted Child*, the authors relate, "Some bright pre-adolescents and adolescents are given adult status too early, and they may later openly critique your friends or expect you to consult with them before you date others" (2007, p. 240).

Adultizing a child confuses their role in the family and forces them to take on responsibility for the well-being of one or both parents. This adult responsibility translates to a lost childhood free of adult worries and problems. That childhood experience can never be replaced. The child may take on this adult role without the adult forcing it upon them. They may ask questions about living arrangements, mortgages, paying the bills. It is important to address them at an age appropriate level and offer reassurance.

Enmeshment occurs when a parent's life satisfaction is dependent upon his or her children's activities and achievements. In these cases, it is difficult to see where the child ends and the parent begins. Newly divorced parents can easily become enmeshed with their child because there is no longer another adult in the home with whom to interact. And sometimes enmeshment happens when parents see children "squandering" opportunities that the parents didn't have but wish they'd had, like piano or drama lessons, and they then push the child to achieve in one or more of those areas (Miller, 1996).

Ways that Children Adapt

Children, in general, seem to adapt in one of four different ways, as identified by the excellent research of Janet Johnston and Linda Campbell (1988). These four main methods by which children deal with parental separation and conflict are a product of age, gender, and temperament. Given the unique qualities of the gifted child, these different approaches to coping may be expressed to a greater degree or intensity. They include the following:

1. Maneuvering – These children become masters at manipulating their parents to get their needs met. Little by little, they learn to take care of themselves first.
2. Equilibrating – These are the children who become diplomats. They are desperately trying to keep everything under control. On the surface, they seem composed, well organized, and competent. However, under the surface, they are likely to be perpetually anxious. They learn to hide their feelings and to seek safe ways out of the parental conflict.
3. Merging – These are the children who often become enmeshed in the conflict. They may side with the parent they are with at the time. They split their identities in half and have little individual sense of themselves. They are usually unwilling to express their own wishes or desires. Thus, they protect each parent and ensure their loyalty to each parent by "merging" with the parent who is present.
4. Diffusing – The highly reactive child responds to the conflict the way they typically respond to other forms of stress. They may appear to shatter emotionally; in other words, they may appear to be emotional disorganized,

emotionally distraught and generally out of emotional control.

Not surprisingly, it has been our observation that the gifted child also copes with the disintegration of the family along these same lines. Because of their intensities, the impact on gifted children may result in more severe reactions.

One must also keep in mind that parents of gifted children in the throes of an unhappy relationship are likely to be depressed and preoccupied. Just when a child may need the parent(s) the most, the parent(s) may be less available, physically or emotionally. Also, parents of gifted children may be inclined to expect their very bright child to be able to handle emotions and concerns competently, since the child has done so well up to this point in time. Their school work has always been great; and before they have been so mature and so competent so far in life.

Additionally, parents in the throes of separating from, and divorcing their partner often misinterpret what a child, especially a young, very bright child, might say. Toddlers who are more advanced in language development use their language skills to help master the separation experience or attempt to control it. When a two year old questions her mother by asking, "Mama hate papa?" the mother grows angry and interprets the statement as proof that the father was indoctrinating the child. Simply because young children have advanced language abilities does not mean they will grasp the complex relationship between their parents.

Maneuvering

Consider the case in which a young man's parents separated. He is a brilliant 16 year old. One parent moved to one state, while the other parent worked for weeks at a time in another state and returned to the home occasionally, where this young man had been left to fend for himself, independently. Although one part of this young man was happy to be left to his own devices, he also engaged in considerable manipulation of his parents, especially his father. He was angry, perfectionistic, and idealistic. He also possessed a strong sense of entitlement, and when the world did not conform to his expectations, he would withdraw. By withdrawing, he escaped into video games, and his academics suffered. Because his father had high expectations of him, his father would travel more often back home to "straighten out his son." While it may not have been conscious, this adolescent managed to maneuver the situation quite well. He got his father's attention.

Equilibrating

Johnny, an eight-year-old boy, is involved in multiple activities that include violin, piano, drum and singing lessons, as well as attending the Sylvan program to help him with his school work. When seen jointly with his mother, Johnny suggested that all these lessons were his dad's ideas. He said his father makes him practice violin for three hours. He gets mad about having to take so many lessons. His days are clearly filled with school and after school activities. Interestingly, when his father brought him to the appointment, Johnny said he doesn't mind all the activities, although he doesn't particularly like singing. He noted that his father talks to him about going to different schools. Johnny didn't seem to express much interest in changing schools, because he would miss his friends.

This child is overly cautious about what he says and does with each of his parents. He is quite aware of the parental conflict and his place in it. He is careful about not disappointing either parent, nor does he want to cause tension because of his awareness of the conflict. He won't call the non-possessing parent from either home. In fact, he seems so eager to please and not disappoint, that when he perceives he has failed one or the other parent, he may take the anger and frustration out on himself. He was in the first and second grade when he got angry and cut himself. When asked why he would hurt himself, he said because his mom got mad at him for doing something. He will also hit himself if he isn't doing as well as he thinks he should in school. There is a lot of pressure being brought to bear on this child by both his parents, and his father in particular.

This is the equilibrating child. This is also the gifted child who is set on making sure everything is fair and equal, to organize things and people, making sure neither parent is upset and taken care of. This is the child who, when you discuss time spent with each parent, will insist on spending equal time with each parent: it would only be fair. Hence, with respect to the parental conflict, the child could simultaneously experience the juxtaposition of different interests and abiding conflicted feelings and seek a solution that would meet the needs of both of his parents.

Merging

Frequently the bright, perfectionistic child is inclined to merge with one parent over the other. Anger at the vagaries of the world, the inequities and unfairness of events can play a significant role in how the gifted child copes with family problems. Out of anger and idealism, the child may not be able to accept that human relationships are ambiguous and that the reasons families disintegrate are equally unclear with no clear guidelines as to who is right or wrong. It is intolerable to think grey when one insists things are black or white, right or wrong. A way out of the conundrum is to "choose sides" and align with one parent. Richard Gardner invoked the term "Parental Alienation syndrome" (PAS) to identify some of these highly aligned children.

Whether there is such a syndrome or not is being debated. However, our observations and experience have convinced us that with the perfectionistic, gifted child, the means of coping with the ambiguity and anger resides in aligning with one parent. Children between the ages of six to 12 or 13 are most vulnerable to this means of coping. Alliances of this type seem to result from a convergence of facts: the child's capacity to conceptualize the whole system of emotional relations in the family, and his or her tendency toward uncompromising views (moral) of the situation. However, unlike PAS, the aligned gifted child may swing back and forth between parents at different times. This is especially true given the emotional intensities seen in some of the children. These are the children who try to make sense of the dispute between their parents and determine who was right, and who was wrong.

Another case reflects just such a pattern of swings in alignment. This 14-year-old boy is highly gifted with both OCD features and Tourettes syndrome (a twice exceptional child). At one point in time, he will be aligned with one parent almost to the exclusion of the other. He will be angry and at times hostile to the excluded parent. Two or three weeks later, he will come in, and his demeanor toward the excluded parent will have done a 180 degree shift, and the parent with whom he was aligned will now be on the outs. It's not always clear what triggers the shift.

Diffusing

There are few good studies of the impact of emotionality on coping with parental divorce. Some studies break down emotionality into two subtypes: positive and negative emotionality. Nowhere can be found research on the presence of emotional overexcitabilities and the impact on coping with crisis. These are the children who react intensely to the disintegration of the family.

For example, two years after their parents divorced, two children ages eight and twelve, both gifted and highly emotional, continued to have difficulties with emotionality. Dramatic, emotional, and highly imaginative--whenever there were changes about to occur with either parent, it was if the world were ending. One parent was moving about 600 miles away, and the thought of changing schools and activities and friends triggered tears and anger in both children as well as meltdowns in one of them.

Another child may create complex fantasies. A ten-year-old boy resolved his loyalty dilemmas by creating a complex fantasy of living with Buck Rogers in a mansion on another planet, and when his parents argued, he would jump in and karate chop them.

The bright, sensitive child may also be quick to sense a parent's sadness and assume the role of caretaker or rescuer.
Parental Influence
All the above styles of coping, whether by the average child or the gifted child, are influenced by parents. High conflict between parents is widely recognized to create added risk for the children. The research literature on children in general tends to suggests that children who adapted more successfully were on the whole, intelligent, attractive, and more skilled

socially. Their self-confidence and more cohesive and independent view of themselves seemed partly to derive from successful achievements and relationships in various other areas of their lives.

One must also keep in mind that, more often than not, gifted children come from gifted parents. Gifted parents also have their own intensities that can aggravate an already difficult situation.

How Parents Can Reduce Risk to Children

In their wonderful book, *Cradles of Eminence*, Victor and Mildred Goertzel (2004) examined the childhoods of famous men and women and wrote the following about eminent people from troubled homes:

> [N]ormality, as evidenced by a lack of internal tension; adequate social, economic, and familial adaptation, and harmonious integration with other individuals at all levels, implies a lack of creativity, imagination, and spontaneity. The comfortable and contented do not ordinarily become creative (p. 134).
>
> Children in these turbulent and explosive homes do not always enjoy life. They suffer intensely at times, and they are deeply capable of suffering since they are sensitive and aware individuals (p. 135).
>
> In the homes that cradle eminence, creativity and contentment are not congenial. Both parents and children are often irritable, explosive, changeable, and experimental. They are prone to depression and exultation. They make terrible mistakes and win wonderful victories (p. 133).

Here are some ways that parents can reduce the mistakes, and maximize victories.

1. Be cooperative. Low-conflict, co-parenting relationships have been linked to better child outcomes. Having a concise "parenting agreement" will help you to avoid conflict.

2. Accept and appreciate your child's uniqueness.

3. It is easy to fall into the trap of parentifying or adultizing your gifted child. Be careful about "too much" sharing of information with your child(ren) about matters that should be managed by the adults. Your gifted child is curious and sensitive. Gifted children are not miniature adults.

4. Children have "big ears" and you can bet they will be listening into conversations and picking up court documents, etc. They glean from the adults around them that something is going on. Don't lie to them, don't patronize them. Be truthful, but also be diplomatic and age appropriate.

5. Do not demean the absent parent to or in front of the children. It is the healthy parent who recognizes the importance of the other parent to the child(ren) and will facilitate the relationship with the other parent.

6. Avoid letting the child get in the middle of disagreements.

7. Be aware of your own intensities, sensitivity, and other such traits that may define you as a gifted adult. As the authors note in *A Parent's Guide to Gifted Children*, "Just as with gifted children, your passion, idealism, concern for quality, perfectionism and impatience may be great strengths, but they can also be hindrances."

This is especially true during the trying times associated with the disintegration of a relationship.

8. Be careful about not living out your own fantasies through your child.

9. Take care of yourself. When marriages and partnerships end, grief and anger follow. That is normal. It is normal to have mixed feelings and to feel several different ways all at once. Sometimes, parents can become caught up in their own misery and difficulties so that the children, who are also living the crisis, get pushed into the background.

10. Communication between separated parents is essential. You may not like each other, but parents are responsible for their children and for creating the environment and opportunities for them to develop in a healthy manner. While parenting styles may differ, expectations from one household to another should overlap. Communicate by email if necessary regarding your kids.

11. Just because there is strife and stress, just because relationships fail and times are hard, just because you make mistakes and are imperfect, does not mean your children will be damaged, will be a failure, or will not achieve.

Take an active interest in how your children are coping with the divorce. Look at the process and effects from your child's point of view. Try to understand their coping style and whether it is working for them or not. If not, gently guide them to a better style of coping. In summary, the single best step you can take is to keep the lines of communication open with your children.

References

Johnston, J. R, & Campbell, L. E. G. (1988). *Impasses of divorce: The dynamics and resolution of family conflict.* New York: Free Press.

Gardner, R. (1992). Parental alienation syndrome: A guide for mental health and legal professionals. Cresskill, NJ: Creative Therapeutics.

Goertzel, V., Goertzel, M.G., Goertzel, T.G. & Hansen, A.M.W. (2004). *Cradles of eminence: Childhoods of more than seven hundred famous men and women,* 2nd edition. Scottsdale: Great Potential Press.

Miller, A. (revised and updated, 1996). *The drama of the gifted child.* New York City: Basic Books

Webb, J.T., Gore, J., Amend, E., & DeVries, A. (2007). *A parent's guide to gifted children.* Scottsdale: Great Potential Press.

SENG President Lori Comallie-Caplan is currently in private practice specializing in therapy and evaluation of gifted children and adolescents in Las Cruces, New Mexico. Mrs. Comallie-Caplan is a Certified Educational Diagnostician and Certified Frasier Talent Assessment Profile Evaluator. She also is a certified SENG (Supporting Emotional Needs of the Gifted) Model Parent Group Facilitator as well as a SENG Model Parent Group Facilitator Trainer. She frequently presents at SENG and NAGC annual conferences.

Marc A. Caplan, PhD, is a clinical psychologist in private practice. With 36 years of experience in the mental health field, Dr. Caplan has an eclectic practice that includes assessment and psychotherapeutic work with children, adolescents and adults. He is one of very few psychologists in New Mexico that specializes in work with gifted children.

Where Does a Pediatric Doctor Fit in the Care of Gifted Children?

By Marianne Kuzujanakis

I wear two hats: One—as a pediatrician. The other—as a parent of a gifted child. To be honest, there are days when neither hat fits comfortably, if at all. There are days when my medical knowledge just isn't enough to understand my child, and other days when being a parent hasn't always provided all the answers.

Can there be a synergy of these two roles?

Gifted kids do not suddenly become gifted on the first day of Kindergarten, nor are they gifted only during school hours. Most, if not all, parents may admit they felt hunches about their child's abilities well before school age. Some parents may have even had concerns or questions about their child's giftedness during these early years, yet they didn't always know to whom to turn. Raising a gifted child can at times be a lonely and demanding journey for parents, and growing up as a gifted child is frequently fraught with challenges. Reaching out for an understanding voice may be difficult. Thus, many parents seek out organizations like SENG, as well as close friends and family members who can offer advice and support.

A sometimes overlooked individual who is ideally

positioned to offer parents advice and support is the child's medical doctor. These doctors may be pediatricians, family practitioners, naturopaths, or other allied health professionals. Many happy parents already find great comfort and advice from their children's doctors, though others, for a variety of reasons, do not. Some parents may never have broached the subject of giftedness with their child's doctor, considering giftedness not a medical issue, or feeling that discussing giftedness is marked with elitism. Doctors may feel likewise, and avoid the topic altogether. Some parents may also recall uncomfortable conversations with their child's doctor or a previous doctor when giftedness was bought up, then quickly dismissed, and that made them hesitate to ever again discuss the subject. Some doctors, upon hearing about a child's giftedness, may simply respond with "That's wonderful. You must be lucky to have such an easy child to raise." Argh.

By the time a child is five years of age, a child has typically seen his or her pediatric doctor a dozen times for healthy visits. With an average physical exam lasting twenty minutes, this amounts to four hours of face-to-face contact in those first five years, then one visit per year thereafter. Each visit is an opportunity – or missed opportunity – to address social, emotional, and developmental issues.

But is it important that pediatric doctors understand and address giftedness?

Medical doctors diagnose and treat a wide variety of acute and chronic medical conditions. Most are highly trained to do their job. Lectures and study about giftedness are not routinely part of the curriculum in medical training programs, yet giftedness can often play a significant role in the health and emotional well being of a gifted child. Reports indicate that doctors usually perform developmental assessments only 50 percent of the time, and these assessments primarily look at children not meeting the minimum standard developmental milestones. Many parents may be equally unaware that there is no specific pediatric medical record code (ICD or DSM) for "gifted." Most doctors are compensated by the codes they indicate in the medical record. Having no specific medical code, many doctors, already overworked and pressed for time, have little incentive to discuss giftedness further.

When a child's gifted needs are not served, the result can be expressed in a physical or emotional symptom. Many gifted children may experience bodily complaints as a result of a mismatch in their educational situation, or due to an unfulfilled emotional or social need. Stomachaches and headaches are common school avoidance symptoms. Eating disorders can be a result of poor self-esteem. Depression and suicidal attempts may result from feeling different or isolated or even bullied. Sensory intensities and the asynchrony of gifted children may be exhibited in extreme ways, sometimes making diagnoses difficult for those without knowledge of giftedness, and resulting in incorrect labeling of the gifted child. In other cases, a medical condition or learning disorder may almost completely hide one's giftedness, as is seen in many twice-exceptional gifted children.

When worrisome health issues present at a pediatric doctor office, and if the doctor has a strong background knowledge of giftedness, he or she will be better positioned to understand and differentiate the symptoms from signs of giftedness, thus resulting in fewer misdiagnoses and fewer inappropriate medical treatments. If a doctor remains unsure of a presenting diagnosis, strong background knowledge of giftedness will still make it far easier to appropriately make any needed referrals, thus finding quicker answers for the parents and child.

Pediatric doctors are drawn into their careers by the thrill of working with children. They are among the most beloved of medical practitioners, and they do not take the privilege of caring for the youngest among us for granted. Many doctors are also gifted, and may understand the developmental paths of their gifted patients. They can be lifesavers for many parents who are anxious and exhausted by the enormous responsibility of raising these intense and complex children.

At the same time, many parents do not feel a need to discuss giftedness with their child's doctor. Some parents feel able to be their own strong supportive advocates for their gifted children, and may also be gifted. Their children may have many friends who are gifted, and the stages of growing up are less bumpy, and more balanced. The personal need to discuss giftedness with one's pediatric doctor in these situations may diminish.

But can parents do something to help make their good interactions better, or to improve their unsatisfying interactions, or even to help other more needy gifted families? If parents of gifted children want or require more from their child's doctor, they do not need to let the status quo remain. They may open an active dialogue about giftedness if they are aware that a doctor's time is limited. Parents can slowly begin a conversation by staying focused on exactly what is needed at each particular visit, and to concisely articulate any specific questions.

Other suggestions for both parents who are already satisfied with the support they receive, and also for parents seeking greater support, include the following:

- Do your homework ahead of time when asking about

topics such as testing, evaluation for a learning disability, consulting for depression, or other specific situation or information need.

- Consider asking your child's doctor if he or she would be willing to allow an informational sheet or brochure to be posted in the office waiting room for other parents. SENG has several brochures, including one made in collaboration with NAGC called "Is My Child Gifted?"

- If needed, gently offer to educate your doctor about giftedness by putting together a brief typed listing of gifted resources such as SENG, NAGC, Davidson Institute, Hoagies Gifted, online parent forums such as GT-Families, TAGFAM (and its associated subgroups), and your state gifted association. If your doctor approves, you may offer to post the list on the waiting room bulletin board.

- If you have a supportive doctor, consider asking your doctor if he or she would be willing to run a local community support group for parents of gifted children. Possibly even suggest having the doctor train with SENG through the SMPG program.

- If you are or become quite comfortable with giftedness, you, too, may consider training as a parent facilitator through SENG and the SMPG program, and then offering your services for other parents of gifted children within your local area.

- Again...start slowly. Very slowly. Consider not just the needs of your child, but also the needs of other families like yours in your community. Some parents may not even be aware of organizations like SENG, and may be highly appreciative of any and all information and support. Start a grassroots gifted revolution!

"Be the change you want to see in the world."
- Mahatma Gandhi

Cultivating a satisfying relationship with your pediatric doctor in ways that fulfill the unique needs of you and your gifted child can be a warm ray of light upon everyone involved. No other professional has the potential to participate in the developmental course of a child for a longer time period. While many pediatric doctors already serve a vital role in the support of the gifted child, there is much more that can be done so all gifted families have similar support. If a professional such as a doctor truly appreciates, understands, and is available to offer advice when the road to adulthood becomes challenging, it can be life changing for a gifted child. By taking an active role in the cultivation of this relationship, every parent has the potential to play an important role in improving the lives of not just their own children, but all gifted families. Start a grassroots gifted revolution!

References

Amend, E.R., & Clouse, R.M. (2007). *The Role of Physicians in the Lives of Gifted Children.* Parenting for High Potential, September, 6-9.

Goerss, J., Clouse, R., & Webb, J. T. (2008). *Health Care Providers Know Little about Gifted Children.* National Psychologist. 16(2),12.

Hayden, T. (1985). *Reaching out to the gifted child: Roles for health-care professions.* New York: American Association for Gifted Children.

Liu, .Y.H, & Lien, J. (2005). *Discovering Gifted Children in Pediatric Practice.* Journal of Developmental and Behavioral Pediatrics. 26, 366-369.

Robinson, N. M., & Olszewski-Kubilius, P. M. (1996) *Gifted and talented children: Issues for pediatricians.* Pediatrics in Review, 17(12), 427-434.

Webb, J.T., Amend, E.R., Webb, N.E., Goerss, J. Beljan, & Olenchak, F.R., (2005*). Misdiagnosis and Dual Diagnoses of Gifted Children and Adults: ADHD, Bipolar, OCD, Asperger's, Depression, and Other Disorders.* Scottsdale, AZ: Great Potential Press.

SENG Director Marianne Kuzujanakis, MD, MPH, is SENG's Medical Liaison and a board-certified pediatrician with long-standing interests in parent and clinician education. She is a primary care pediatrician in Massachusetts and a clinical instructor, both through Harvard Medical School and as the course director of a local clinician-training program for pediatricians.

One More Door...a personal challenge

By Sheri Plybon

I recently began a new SENG Model Parent Group of ten parents. In preparation for our discussion of chapter four of *A Parent's Guide to Gifted Children*, Motivation, Enthusiasm, and Underachievement, I wanted to be able to present an additional short piece about Abraham Maslow's Hierarchy of Needs.

Maslow was a psychologist who studied, among other topics, healthy personalities, peak experiences, and the journey to self-actualization (being all one can be). The authors of *A Parent's Guide to Gifted Children* explain Maslow's Hierarchy of Needs theory as "a sequence of eight needs that reflect human development from infancy to adulthood. These needs evolve from the most basic human needs to the most advanced, and those needs that are the most basic almost always take priority over the more advanced ones" (p. 68). Here are some thoughts on his theory as it applies to the four advanced levels. Motivation is driven by both external and internal forces. We personally choose to follow these to accomplish a task, and this may lead to what some call underachievement. Yet, in *A Parent's Guide to Gifted Children*, the *Need to Know and Understand* (Level 5) describes the intensity that children (and adults) have regarding learning. It has moved from extrinsic school / work related learning to the exploration of topics of personal (intrinsic) motivation. Approval or acceptance from others is no longer necessary. From an educational standpoint, a child may appear to be stubborn and non-cooperative, and seen as a problem. Clarification of motivation may help teachers and others understand the difference between an underachiever and a non-producer.

This personal sense of inquiry follows to *Level 6 – Aesthetic Needs*. Passion is a key term at this level, and an individual's sense of the aesthetic flows to passion, and this in turn becomes the change from "doing" to "being." To this point, all six levels of the hierarchy have begun the assimilation of a personal change which Maslow describes as the development of *Level 7 - Self-Actualization*, or self-fulfillment, realizing one's potential.

Finally we come to Level 8 – *Self-Transcendence*, moving from personal development / gratification to the need to help others reach their potential, and to improve the world.

Assume you have a special visualization tool that allows you to watch a gifted child's growth from infancy through adolescence to adulthood, and that you could clearly see Kazimierz Dabrowski's intensities overlay upon the Maslow Hierarchy.

First, you would see an infant so alert to the world around him that you would believe that this child has a personal communication with nature. Early reading or hands-on experimentation drives a passion for learning. In adolescence, the cognitive processes of the content – the "what" – then are replaced by the intellectual and philosophical drive to understand the "why," which ultimately becomes the realization of potential in the "what if" (adolescent / adult). Intermingled in all of this growth is the understanding that knowledge is power: the ultimate is power for good, and a sense of high moral judgment. If gifted individuals accept the knowledge of their power, and find the balance of sensitivity experienced in the Dabrowskian intensities, they will move towards self–transcendence.

A new door to personal understanding can be opened. The following is a short list of thoughts and exercises that one can walk through, which will enlighten the path to understanding the gifted.

Developing Self-Actualization: Moving towards Transcendence

- Experience each moment fully, vividly and with total concentration
- Think of life as a process of choices, your choices
- Listen to your Self; trust your inner voice
- Take responsibility for yourself
- Dare to be different, nonconforming, real
- Do what you do with joy, and do it well
- Set up conditions that will allow more peak experiences, perceive the world and life positively
- Experience life with awe and wonder
- Seek periods of privacy for intense concentration and meditation
- Open up to yourself, identify your defenses, and find the courage to fire them up
- Make your goal to have access to all of your life, all of your potential, to be who you are

References & Resources

Maslow, A. H. (1970). *Motivation and personality* (2nd. Ed). New York: Harper & Row.

Webb, J. T., Gore, J. L., Amend, E, R. & DeVries A, R. (2007). *A parent's guide to gifted children.* Arizona: Great Potential Press.

SENG Director and President-Elect Sheri Plybon is a SENG Model Parent Group Facilitator and Trainer, and she has been a Gifted Specialist for 28+ years in public education, K-12. Her passion for understanding giftedness was inspired by her three gifted children and by her own personal experiences in gifted education. Ms. Plybon earned her Bachelor of Science in Behavioral Science from Loretto Heights College, and a Master's Degree in Educational Administration from Colorado State University.

Part IV

First-Person Gifted

Resilient Hispanic Women

By Rosina M. Gallagher

Resilience can be defined as the innate ability to cope with adversity. The research literature identifies four common attributes of resilience: social competence, problem-solving, autonomy and a sense of purpose and future (Benard, 1991, 97).* In my professional experience, I have had the privilege of engaging many Latin-American women, in their teens, middle and late adult years, who, armed with these attributes, have risen above adverse conditions to emerge strong adults leading gratifying lives.

I think of Ana María, a thirteen-year old, whose family comes from rural Tegucigalpa, Honduras, and has resided in a large, mid-western city for 10 years. Ana María is beginning her eighth grade in a magnet gifted center. She has distinguished herself for overall performance and high aptitude in math and science. Last spring she was among a group invited to meet Astronaut Commander Eileen Collins. But Ana María has also learned to become a public advocate. At the end of her sixth grade, she volunteered to testify at the State Senate to support the reinstitution of legislation and funding for gifted programs. In her 30-second testimony, she stated, "I was born in Honduras but have been raised in this great city. My father is a welder. He has two jobs. My mother works at home and volunteers at school. They don't speak much English but work very hard. My brother just received a four-year scholarship to attend a private high school academy. I came here to thank you for supporting the bilingual gifted program at my school. Many students like my brother and me would not have had an opportunity to do well without this program. Today I speak to you from this side of the Senate floor, but tomorrow I hope to be in one of your seats."

I recall Graciela, a girl from a humble Mexican background who graduated from a public magnet gifted center with a four-year scholarship to a private college-prep high school. Midway in her sophomore year, her father suffered a back-injury at work. Her mother spoke only Spanish and had to care for her husband and a younger son. To provide shelter and food for a family of four, Graciela kept two jobs, one as a clerical assistant in a radio station after school and one on weekends at a fast-food restaurant. To relieve the pressure of maintaining a minimum "B" average, Graciela describes what sustained her. "I prayed every day. I also went back to my teachers at my elementary school. They just listened to me, offered advice, a nice lunch or help with my projects. Together we came up with the idea for mother to make fresh tamales for my dad to sell at a corner stand at 6:00 a.m. every morning." Graciela graduated from the private academy and is now a second year scholarship student at the University of Southern California planning to become an attorney.

After speaking at a recent conference I met tearful parents who confessed being "undocumented." Their daughter had just graduated with high honors from an urban public high school, but, lacking the magic "nine-digit number," could not apply for college scholarships or financial aid. Thanks to supportive and dedicated teachers and counselors who raise funds annually for token scholarships for undocumented graduates, and earnings from her waitress job, Aurora will attend her first year at a community college. "Praying, working hard, and talking to people bring us hope!" explain the parents.

Vivid still is Margarita's story. At age 10 she was selling fruit juices in her native Durango, Mexico, to help her single mother support a family of six. At age 15 her mother passed away. To sustain herself and four siblings, Margarita "emigrated" to the U.S, having to lie about her age to find a job. She recalls, "I always thought there was something wrong with me because I never went to school and had difficulty learning to read…I still can't speak English very well." Married shortly thereafter to a husband who curtailed her independence, she dedicated herself to caring for siblings and eventually four offspring. But she struggled to pursue the dream of becoming a beautician by cutting and styling hair for neighbors in the basement of her home, unbeknownst to her husband. Although apprehensive about her competencies, she also became an active participant in school. "I learned so much, and found I could encourage other mothers by sharing my life experiences." Today, Margarita's siblings are gainfully employed, several with high school diplomas. Her children are recipients of scholarships; the eldest daughter is finishing business administration, a second is in her sophomore year at a private university, a son attends Culver in Indiana and the youngest will join her brother at the private academy this school year. And…Margarita has just inaugurated her own beauty parlor, "Dreams," which family helped her convert from a run-down tire shop! Her husband now comments, "I'm glad you didn't let me stand in your way, sweetheart!"

Finally, there is a colleague's struggle to develop her cultural identity and professional goals. Born in USA from an

American father and a Colombian mother, Sofía went to study Spanish in Santa Fe de Bogotá. She married a Colombian teacher and became a bilingual teacher herself as the family returned to the U.S. Sofía joined a magnet center for gifted Hispanic English learners and zealously supported its development for 16 years. Inspired by this venture, she eventually completed her doctorate in education and is currently becoming the principal of an elementary school in a Hispanic neighborhood.

The women in these brief case studies reflect resilience and embody some of the cultural values Hispanics hold dear. The unquestioning sense of responsibility for family, strong spiritual beliefs and respect for hard work and personal relationships are clear threads, as is their evolving role. Salient also are elements which have helped these women attain their goals: high expectations, supportive relationships and increased self-efficacy. SENG groups have certainly proven a rich forum where Hispanic women may begin to explore their own sense of self, history and direction.

*Benard, B. and Marshall, K. (Spring, 1997). A framework for practice: Tapping innate resilience. Research/Practice, Minneapolis: University of Minnesota Center for Applied Research and Educational Improvement.

Former SENG President Rosina Gallagher, Ph.D., was born and raised in Mexico through early adolescence. Her 30-year career includes being a psychologist and administrator in the Chicago Public Schools, and she is currently president of the Illinois Association for Gifted Children. Dr. Gallagher is the co-author of Educando Hijos Exitosos *(with James T. Webb, Great Potential Press) and numerous articles.*

The Hardships of Being Gifted in Culturally Diverse Populations

By Tiombe-Bisa Kendrick

While glancing at the Black Entertainment Television's (BET) Honors Awards Show recently, I was taken aback by a comment made by infamous and legendary film director, Spike Lee. He shared with the crowd directly in front of him, along with millions of viewers across the nation, that "parents are the biggest dream killers." I immediately halted what I was doing at the time and thought to myself, Spike Lee is so right! You see, in my practice as a school psychologist in one of the most diverse cities in the country, and as a member of the African-American community, I have watched gifted and talented children and young adults from diverse backgrounds postpone or give up entirely on their dreams and aspirations. I have seen so many people from diverse populations throughout my life end up squandering their potential. I often wonder about what seems to be far too many African-American young people giving up so easily on their dreams.

As it turns out, many times, these individuals face pressures from their families, peers, and community to pursue career paths that do not match their actual life goals, gifts, or talents. In many non-majority cultures, being classified as gifted and talented can create a life-long struggle with adversity that is unfamiliar to those outside of that particular culture. Emotionally, many of these individuals find themselves maneuvering between two completely different worlds that are extremely hard to bring into harmony. Often, they experience a constant inner battle that includes struggles with loyalty issues. Loyalty to families, peers, and community is often emphasized as very important in non-majority cultures. For example, gifted and talented youth from African-American backgrounds will often experience the painful and stressful experience of having to choose between being loyal to peers, family, and community, or pursuing their dreams. These individuals may experience relentless feelings of guilt directed at their families and communities. These feelings are created by their very difficult choice to take a different path in life from the one prescribed for them by those who are closest both socially and emotionally. In many instances, these individuals will come to realize that pursuing their dreams, gifts, and talents may isolate them from the very people who have supported them for their entire lives. In other instances, they will realize that their families and communities both expect great things from them and feel they are owed something significant for all their years of support. For example, someone who is expected to give back financially to community or family, but chooses not to, may be viewed in a very negative light and forced into isolation. Being isolated, either by force or necessity, can become very emotionally draining and very painful, especially for people from diverse backgrounds. As a result, many may end up engaging in destructive behaviors as a way to cope with the pain.

In addition to facing the additional pressures from their

families, peers, and communities, diverse individuals must also contend with the many pressures of the society in which they live. Many times, these individuals may experience barriers, such as discrimination and a lack of resources needed to perfect their gifts and talents, thus placing them in a disadvantaged position in a very competitive society! Often these individuals are aware of the injustices present in society that are responsible for many of the barriers that block them from reaching their potential.

Educators and mental health professionals working with this population must focus on providing them with support and their communities and families with education. Gifted and talented individuals must learn effective coping skills, which may act as a buffer when the pain lands at their doorstep. Their families and communities must learn to put aside their anxieties and replace them with support, sacrifice, and understanding. There are too many gifted and talented individuals from diverse backgrounds giving up on their dreams or lacking the resources to hone their gifts and talents, and it's a real shame! I strongly believe we must increase awareness about this issue in our schools, colleges, and among mental health professionals in order to free individuals, communities, and families from creating a silent lifetime of pain.

SENG Director Tiombe-Bisa Kendrick is a nationally certified school psychologist and has been employed with the Miami-Dade County Public School District as a school psychologist since 2005. In 2007, she was both appointed to the NAGC

Diversity/Equity Committee and was awarded a grant by the National Association of School Psychologists (NASP) Children Fund Inc. to establish a resource center specifically designed for gifted students from culturally and linguistically diverse backgrounds.

The Best of Both Worlds: On Being Indian

By Vidisha Patel

One of the blessings of living in sunny Florida at this time of year is that we host numerous visitors. This year has been particularly busy with visits from relatives coming to Florida for the first time. Having just returned from a trip to India with my own children, our conversations have centered around life as Indian immigrants: both the joys and the challenges.

Perspectives on Fitting In

My family immigrated to the United States over forty years ago in search of better job opportunities for my parents and educational opportunities for us, the children. This was also the case for many of my cousins. We were fortunate in that our parents taught us how to assimilate into the western culture while still maintaining our comfort and familiarity with our heritage. We returned to India on a regular basis, maintained a level of fluency in our native languages, and continued our cultural traditions. Unlike other immigrants, we did not reject our heritage, nor did we hang onto it to the exclusion of embracing western traditions. We thought we did a great job of assimilating into the United States.

Yet, we were different. We spent much of our lives trying

to fit in with our peers, both in America and in India. In reality, we didn't fit into either place. In America, we looked different, ate different food, and lived with different rules from our peers. In India, we were singled out as having been "Americanized" with funny accents and an inability to speak Marathi and Gujarati correctly. It was only at a much older age that we were able to recognize and appreciate the benefits of growing up across two cultures.

Our parents were extremely protective of us. They always wanted to know where we were and what we were doing. There was no privacy in our home. At any given time, there would be several extra people in the house visiting for a few days. Our grandmothers came from India annually and stayed for several months at a time. Frequently, we would give up our rooms for relatives or share the room with them.

We ate traditional Indian food six nights out of seven. Indian food is typically eaten with your hands, so when we had friends over, not only were we explaining what the food was, but we also had to teach them how to eat with their hands. Some of our friends found it fascinating, and others chose not to come again!

Socially, when our friends were going to parties or out to the movies and having sleepovers, we were usually not allowed to go. Our parents didn't see the need for us to go out on the weekends and certainly not until late at night.

For our parents, educating us was the most important gift they could provide. They wanted us to study hard, learn to think laterally, and do well. We were also expected to learn musical instruments, play sports, and read. In turn, they were willing to provide the support to ensure that we would be able to experience these things.

They would drive us to activities, help us to study if we

needed it, and buy us supplies to ensure that we could complete projects successfully.

Spending money frivolously on fashionable clothes or toys was not considered a good use of funds. We were not encouraged to follow the trends of fashion, and we did not have the latest toys or games. If these games were educational, then it was a different matter.

Summer camp and summer jobs were not an option. Most summers, we went back to India and visited our relatives. We had private instruction in our native language, and we always had lots of books to read and summer homework. We also traveled throughout India to visit a few sites and many relatives. As we became older, we were told that we could get a summer job as long as it was educational. Our parents were not interested in our getting a job to earn money if we were not going to be learning something from the job. This limited our summer jobs to research fellowships and internships. Again, this was based on a firm belief that the parents' role is to educate their children, and that work for the sake of "pocket money" was not acceptable.

From my parents' perspective, they were sacrificing their lives to give us the best opportunities that they were capable of providing. From our perspective, we were struggling to fit in. It was challenging to try to fit in to a culture that valued independence when we lived half our lives in a culture that valued interdependence.

We found ourselves living a dual life. In school, we did our best to fit in by imitating our peers. As soon as we stepped into our homes, we were transported to India. We spoke Marathi and Gujarati at home much of the time, ate Indian food for almost all of our meals, and followed the cultures and traditions that our family was accustomed to. Since we didn't know anything else, we quickly adapted to this way of life.

Standing Outside the Candy Shop Window

Indian immigrant parents tend to be extremely protective of their children. Children are considered a gift of god and are to be nurtured, protected, and educated to the fullest extent. These parents, in turn, work hard to achieve the means to educate their children and to provide them with the best opportunities in life. It is expected that the children will study hard, be successful, and ultimately take care of their parents when they age. Socializing is frequently limited to family gatherings or parties where the entire family is invited. Rarely do Indian immigrant parents allow their children to go out late with friends on weekends, as might be typical for an American teenager. Marriages are often arranged or 'introduced," so dating is also not encouraged.

Academics are the primary focus of life for Indian children. They are expected to study and earn good grades. Diligence, time, and effort are rewarded, and laziness is not accepted. The result is a lonely existence for an Indian immigrant adolescent in America. It is almost like standing outside the candy shop window, watching your peers buying and eating whatever they like. It accentuates the differences rather than bridging the cultural gap.

Benefits of Being Different

However, it is also important to recognize that there are benefits to being "different." Indian immigrant families are usually extremely nurturing and supportive. The challenges that come with immigrating to a new country and planting roots create a strong bond within families and other members of the immigrant community. The greater immigrant community provides an extended support network, both socially and during challenging times. This network extends across the country as well. Wherever we go, we can find family, friends, or friends of friends who are welcoming.

Education is highly valued and encouraged. If children demonstrate proficiency in any subject area, they are encouraged to pursue it further. Parents will go to great lengths to allow their children to excel in whatever area they show promise.

What I Have Learned

Giftedness adds another layer of challenges when combined with the Indian immigrant experience. Gifted children frequently feel different and misunderstood. Cultural differences only add to the sense of isolation. Indian parents typically don't talk about feelings or worry about their child's sense of isolation. The focus is primarily on success in academics. So, if a gifted Indian child shows signs of feeling depressed or frustrated, it will frequently be glossed over. Indian parents are less likely to seek assistance from outside professionals. There is a pride that prevents them from taking their child to receive outside help. They would rather solve the problem internally and quietly. Indian parents may be in denial that their child has a challenge, and these challenges would rarely be discussed outside the home. If only parents would speak to their peers, they might learn that they are not alone, that there are other children and families who experience similar difficulties. Even if they don't want to speak to a professional, they can get some comfort from the knowledge that they are not alone.

As a first generation immigrant and the parent of two gifted children, I have learned several important lessons.

- It's okay to be different.
- Everyone faces challenges.
- Recognizing the need for help and asking for help shows strength of character.
- Culture matters.
- Retain your culture and integrate into the society in which you live.

As immigrants, we can and do have the best of both worlds. We are extremely fortunate to have two cultures and traditions to draw from. We can choose the best of both worlds to live our lives to the fullest.

Vidisha Patel has a doctorate of Education in Counseling Psychology and practices as a therapist in Sarasota, Florida, where much of her work is with gifted children and their families, with a focus on stress and anxiety. Dr. Patel holds an MBA from Columbia University and worked in finance on Wall Street and overseas before obtaining her doctorate in psychology. Dr. Patel is the mother of two gifted children.

Rising to Juilliard:
A Profile of a Gifted Young Actor
By SENG

Jeremy Tardy knew he wanted to be an actor when he was five years old. At first glance, it might look as though his path from those early years to his being a member of Juilliard's drama class of 2013—one of only eighteen freshmen—was a charmed one. After all, by the time he was in sixth grade, he was acting in Milwaukee's First Stage Children's Theater productions, in which child actors typically are in twenty performances per show for runs of three weeks to paying audiences. In high school, he performed in plays by Oscar Wilde, Molière, and Shakespeare, including landing the lead roles of Othello and Macbeth. He won awards and scholarships and gave the commencement speech at his public high school graduation ceremony.

However, Jeremy is the first to say that his path has been far from easy. "I had to sacrifice a lot to reach my goal of getting into Juilliard," he says. "First, I spent a lot of time doing plays throughout high school and middle school, many times sacrificing grades. I faced a lot of skepticism in my pursuits, especially being a young black actor, and even more in auditioning for Juilliard."

Everyone knows how to get to Carnegie Hall (*practice,*

practice, practice), but is practice enough to get to Juilliard, especially from the north side neighborhood of Milwaukee, Wisconsin?

Mentors and Family Support

Karen Arnold, in her fourteen-year study of high school valedictorians, *Lives of Promise*, found that many gifted students require adult mentoring and scaffolding to help them to make the transition from academic success to a career that is right for them. Otherwise, these students may view college narrowly, as "vocational training for upward mobility" rather than a step toward a personally satisfying and meaningful career.

In Jeremy's case, actors and instructors at Milwaukee's First Stage Children's Theater Academy prepared him not only for auditions but also for what it is really like to make a living as an actor, giving him an inside look at the profession he plans to enter. One of these mentors, John Maclay, Academy Director, says of Jeremy, "He has great instincts as an actor, which are complemented by one of the strongest work ethics I have ever seen in a young actor. He is smart, kind, passionate, collaborative, and fearless."

While he credits Maclay and First Stage's Academy Headmaster, Laura DeMoon, for their support and guidance, Jeremy says his most important mentors have been his mother and grandmother: "They are my spiritual and religious foundation and have helped me so much. Without them I could not be here today. My family has always supported me in acting. They have come to all my shows—many times more than once—and they continue to support me in my goals."

In terms of screen and stage influences, Jeremy's favorite male and female actors are Denzel Washington, Marlon

Brando, Angela Bassett, and Meryl Streep. He says, "I have seen most of their works, and I truly admire what they have done on film. Denzel Washington has most influenced me as he is a leading black actor who works against many stereotypes that the film industry portrays with other black actors."

A Passion for Acting and Life

Finding and working with knowledgeable mentors is important for gifted youth, but, as the authors of *Talented Teenagers: The Roots of Success and Failure* remind us, "No teenager will develop talent unless he or she enjoys working in the talent area."

Why does Jeremy love acting? "This is a question that I constantly ask myself," he says, "and one that can only be answered by getting on stage. Many times I feel that the stress, frustration, and work that go into performing are not worth doing, but the blissful feeling of being on stage and giving my heart and soul to the audience makes me want to do it all over again."

His performance ritual is music: "I love music, especially soul music. There is so much passion in the songs of soul singers like Al Green, Marvin Gaye, James Brown, Tina Turner, Nina Simone, and Curtis Mayfield that makes you *feel*. I listen to this music many times before performances. It is something that always infuses me with passion, and I try to emulate this through acting. One needs only to listen to these singers to understand what I mean."

He says that having intensity of emotion is a valuable asset for an actor: "I must be emotionally available to my fellow actors and to my audience. I must be able to have a deep emotional connection to the characters that can only come from being an emotional person. In my training here at Juilliard, I am learning to heighten all my senses as an actor so that I will be much more sensual in life and on stage."

In addition to passion and emotional intensity, Jeremy also displays intellectual curiosity: "I am a very curious person. I love to read books and plays, as well as biographies and autobiographies. I always want to know more."

His Biggest Challenge

"We learned to place less importance on what this society thinks of us, and more [on] what we think of ourselves..." ~ *And Still We Rise*

Jeremy knew early on that his inner drive set him apart from many around him:

From an early age I was driven to get out of the financial and environmental circumstances that I was born into. Most kids focused on just being children and the things children do, but always, in the back of my mind, I felt that I was wasting time in getting myself to where I wanted to be. Although I had a very nice and full childhood, I did not indulge in most things that kids my age were into. Many times I chose to stick to doing what I love to do as a means to rise out of my circumstances.

The biggest challenge I have faced was the challenge of staying on the right track as a teenager with everything that is happening in our world and the things I have been exposed to. I have had many friends get caught up in the street life and the trouble that comes with it. My biggest challenge was to stay out of it, and it was certainly a challenge.

With this biggest challenge behind him, Jeremy can now focus on setting new goals and getting used to his new home: "This is a moving city with so much culture, style, and noise. There is never a dull night here in New York, as there are always places to see."

He is currently working on a show called *The Less Than Human Club*. "I am very excited about it," he says. "Although becoming a student here at Juilliard was a big goal for me, my bigger goal is to make a successful career in mainstream film and theater. I would also love to perform at the Globe Theatre in England and to travel the world, spreading my craft."

For Further Reading

And Still We Rise: The Trials and Triumphs of Twelve Gifted Inner-City Students, by Miles Corin (Harper Perennial, 2001)

Lives of Promise: What Becomes of High School Valedictorians, by Karen Arnold (Jossey-Bass Publishers, 1995)

Talented Teenagers: The Roots of Success and Failure, by Mihaly Csikszentmihalyi, Kevin Rathunde, and Sam Whalen (Cambridge University Press, 1996)

The Juilliard School: http://www.juilliard.edu/

First Stage Children's Theater: http://www.firststage.org/

Under the Spell of Words

By Angela Arenivar

Instead of mounting Backstreet Boys posters on my bedroom wall when I was a teenager, I opted to cover my wall with columns of words like "borborygmus" and "catarrhal" and "otorhinolaryngology." More than anything at the age of thirteen, I wanted to compete in the Scripps National Spelling Bee in Washington, D.C. As I began envisioning myself on the stage at Nationals, I decided that I was going to live, eat, and breathe spelling. A mischievous child, I often played with my Alpha Bits cereal during breakfast. On sunny days, my concept of going outside to play entailed writing words on the sidewalk with chalk. Whenever I could, I would incorporate my expanding vocabulary into everyday conversation and into school writing assignments.

"M'ija, no estudie tanto" (do not study too much), my father would say. I would stay in my room for countless hours, committing as many words as I could to memory. My dad would interrupt my study sessions only to tell me that it was time to eat lunch or dinner.

My parents received a third grade education in Mexico. Because they wanted their children to have access to more educational opportunities, they immigrated to the United States in 1977. Having lived the first five years of my life as a

Spanish-speaker, I became particularly intrigued with words when I learned English in kindergarten.

Years later, when an Amarillo Globe-News reporter asked to speak with my parents after I qualified for the National Spelling Bee in Washington D.C., I responded that they did not speak much English. The reporter asked how I learned "all those words" if my parents did not understand English. I merely shrugged. I remember thinking, "Were my parents supposed to help me? Do other kids' parents help them?"

Growing up, I was called "weirdo" and "nerd" by my peers. One classmate in particular regularly called me a "freak of nature." As I became more interested in spelling, someone told me that if Michelle the genius never made it to Nationals, then neither would I.

Even though I felt out of place with my classmates, my teachers made me feel like I belonged. They assured me that I was intelligent, and they encouraged me to cultivate my interest in writing.

Mrs. Cooksey, my fourth grade teacher, persuaded me to compete in the fourth grade spelling bee, which I won. That experience sparked a sense of determination inside of me. Although there were negative influences around me, I had to drown out those voices and listen to the voice that was within me. My inner voice compelled me to do everything in my power to compete in the National Spelling Bee.

When I competed in the Scripps National Spelling Bee for the first time in 1998, I finally felt like I truly belonged with my peers. We were all verbophiles; therefore, we were all popular. People who did not love words were the "freaks" in our spelling clique. And this time no one was going to insult me and get away with it. Or maybe they could if they used a really obscure word – I might allow that. We sensed each other's tension on the stage. We felt each other's pain when the dreaded ding from the bell dashed our dream of winning the bee.

Traveling to Washington D.C. opened my eyes to the infinite possibilities that existed for my life. The Grand Hyatt where the contest was held was exponentially more luxurious than the Motel 6s my family and I frequented in the summers on our way to Mexico. For the first time in my life, I flew in an airplane and rode in a metro. Seeing the White House in person, and not as a backdrop on the news, left me speechless. I realized that if I worked hard, I could make my dreams come true.

I was just living my everyday life as a speller when Jeff Blitz and Sean Welch contacted me in 1999 about an opportunity to be a subject in their film about spelling bees. Because I competed in the Scripps National Spelling Bee in 1998, they hoped I would advance as an eighth-grader. Jeff and Sean filmed my regional spelling bee victory, which qualified me for Nationals once more. After a few years passed, I thought nothing would ever become of the project.

To my surprise, in 2002 I found out that the film *Spellbound* had been nominated for an Academy Award. The documentary presented the stories of seven other Scripps National Spelling Bee qualifiers from across the country.

Being a featured subject in *Spellbound* presented me with my fifteen minutes of fame. When I was in graduate school, I accidentally hit a cyclist named David with my car.

After I pulled over to the side of the road, David was naturally upset. In addition to the expletives he hurled at me, he asked me if I was paying attention to where I was going.

"I'm so sorry! Are you okay?" I said.

"Oh, my—YOU'RE ANGELA FROM SPELLBOUND!"

I paused. I didn't know what to say.

"Yes, but, um, are you okay?"

"Just a little bruise on my thigh. You can barely even see it, really. What are you doing in Albuquerque?"

What if I had irreparably damaged this total stranger's thigh? Were we really having a conversation about Spellbound after I had just hit him with my car? I didn't know whether to feel guilty that I ran into him, or guilty that we were talking about my experience in the spelling bee.

David said there was no need to call my insurance company. He said I could repay him by editing some of his essays for his English classes. Since it was the least I could do, I gave David a ride home. We talked about my experience in the film and what my future plans were.

Unbelievable, I know, but David's last words to me were, "It was nice to meet you, Angela!"

In order to promote Spellbound, I traveled to Chicago to be on the Oprah Winfrey Show and to Los Angeles to be on the Orlando Jones Show. When I studied in Spain during my junior year in college, I was invited to speak at a school on a military base in Stuttgart, Germany. All of this happened simply because I set out to accomplish my dream of becoming a spelling bee champion.

I now realize that being a freak of nature has been a blessing. I competed in the National Spelling Bee two years in a row. I took Latin for fun in college. I studied in Spain for a semester and have been afforded other travel opportunities. Now I am living my everyday life sharing my love of language as a Spanish teacher. To supplement my lessons, I have written songs to help my students learn words in Spanish.

Looking back on the question that the Amarillo Globe News reporter asked me, I wish I had told her that the most valuable linguistic gift my parents bestowed upon me was the Spanish language. The runner-up of the regional spelling bee misspelled "cabaña" by spelling it with a y. Thanks to my knowledge of the Spanish language, I knew to omit the "y" and was consequently given my winning word. Knowing Spanish also helped me with many of the Latin-based words I encountered in my studies.

While my parents were not capable of helping me with my homework when I was growing up, they always supported me in my endeavors and encouraged me to succeed. In spite of their third grade education, they educated me in ways no textbook ever could. Even though my parents could not fathom why I chose to spend so many hours studying words, they supported me.

Thanks, Mom, for letting me play with my Alpha Bits. And I'll try not to study so much, Dad.

Angela Arenivar was a Scripps National Spelling Bee finalist featured in the Oscar-nominated documentary Spellbound. *She went on to study at Texas A&M University, where she graduated with a Bachelor of Arts in Spanish in May 2007. Arenivar obtained her Master of Arts degree in Spanish at the University of New Mexico in May 2009.*

Her blog, "Okay, so it's heleoplankton. Bee happy," can be found at http://angelainspellbound.blogspot.com.

Through His Eyes and
Through His Mother's Eyes

By Joseph Hughes and Holly Hughes

"I didn't grow up gifted, at least not by name. I grew up being asked what was wrong with me."~ Joseph Hughes, age 19

They always said he was one of the brightest kids in the class.

Right before they sent him to the principal's office.

Introduction

Joseph Hughes once read more than 1,000 books to win a first grade contest.

A high achiever, they all said.

In elementary school, he'd complete class assignments – perfectly – before the other kids.

But he'd quickly find himself in trouble for having done it before the teacher even reviewed the instructions. Impulsive, they all said.

A math whiz, Joe could quickly solve the toughest problems. But he got F after F, simply because he wouldn't show his work properly. A non-conformist, they all said.

And that's when the wheels on Joe's life began to wobble.

His intellect far exceeded most of those around him,

including some of his teachers. Unfortunately, it also far exceeded his emotional development.

Joe became an outcast among his peers, and a struggle for his teachers. He got down on himself, wondering why *he* was always wrong, just because he saw things differently. His pain was deep and profound, eroding both his confidence and his motivation. Which made school, and learning, a horrible torture.

It was only in high school that Joe was "diagnosed" as gifted, a label neither he nor his parents were initially eager to embrace. While others assumed that "gifted" meant compliant and high-achieving, Joe came to understand that not only did he have a *desire* to do things very differently, he had a burning *need*.

At about 16, Joe's parents discovered SENG – *Supporting Emotional Needs of the Gifted.*

"It was like walking through a portal into an amazing new world," Joe's mom, Holly, said. For the Hughes family, SENG became "the best repository of information on the topic, especially the *human* side," Holly remembers. From books and articles, to networking opportunities, to supportive conferences, SENG helped the Hughes family make sense of the inexplicable.

Speaking of portals into strange new lands, Joe completed his GED, entered college, and published a 520-page fantasy fiction novel he first outlined in the sixth grade. *Armorica* is the story of a land "on the brink of destruction, held at the throat by daemons and their cohorts." Sounds like a place with which Joseph Hughes might have some familiarity.

Here is Joe's story, in his own words.

Through His Eyes...

Hello. My name is Joseph Hughes, and I am 19 years old. You are probably asking, "Who are you, and why am I bothering to read this article?" Well, to begin with, the fact that you are reading this publication probably means you care about or are interested in the gifted.

I didn't grow up gifted, at least not by name. I grew up being asked what was wrong with me. People treated me like I was an idiot, at least that's how it felt to me. I had the "privilege" of going to private schools where "everyone is gifted." And I was the misfit because I would not do *what* they wanted *the way* they wanted. The world I grew up in had no idea what giftedness looks like—unless it is compliant and achievement focused. In me, all they saw was a problem kid who needed to be properly disciplined or given pills for ADHD.

This did not work so well.

In the beginning my grades were really good. I worked hard and wanted to impress my parents and make people proud of me. In first grade, we had a competition to read the most books in the year. I read 1046 books, and the runner up read 700-800. But then something started to go wrong. I became an angry kid who hated life and everyone in it because nothing I did ever felt good enough. All I felt anyone wanted from me was results, and that had nothing to do with who I was.

As middle school rolled around, things only became worse, and I was tagged the class problem. My classmates would laugh at me, and whenever something went wrong, fingers pointed my way. Teachers wouldn't even bother checking facts before kicking me out. It was an academically rigorous prep school with rigid standards; while everyone said I "should be able to do the work," I wouldn't do the mountains of homework I found meaningless.

Then came high school. I actually enjoyed a lot about the school and got along with most of my teachers. But after one math teacher gave me F after F simply because I couldn't properly show my work, I stood up, left and never went back into that class again. Supposedly, I'm "gifted" in math.

I left high school and got a GED, convinced that college would be better. It seemed like the other students saw me as weird—I was so much younger—and that made me uncomfortable. I didn't feel I belonged there, either.

My life then suffered a serious, traumatic blow that changed me forever. But it's also how my mother finally discovered what was "wrong" with me. She always tried hard to help me but only now stumbled on the answer. I was gifted – not gifted like sit-straight-in-your-chair-getting-all-As gifted but gifted like really different in the way I look at everything and feel about everything. I first learned about this strange new "gifted world" through SENG, and it was at a SENG conference that I first met people who felt like me, people who seemed to understand me and with whom I connected in a whole, new way.

That led to an introduction to a wonderful lady. Sue Jackson, founder of the Daimon Institute for the Highly and Profoundly Gifted, saved my life, and I am beyond grateful for what she has done for me. Sue has helped me make sense of it all.

Now, I hope my story might help others. I want to say there is nothing *wrong* with us—it's just who we are, and it may not fit with where *you* are and what you want us to be doing. Like when I should have been doing schoolwork from middle school upward, do you know what I did instead? I wrote, rewrote and edited a 600-page manuscript. My fantasy fiction novel, *Armorica*, which was published in 2010. What my teachers and peers criticized as a petty distraction is easily my greatest accomplishment, and I didn't do any of it in school.

So, believe in your kids and what they do. Try to accept our differentness, that being gifted can sometimes look like a lot of other things, some of which aren't so good. And trust us. We know more than you might think.

Through His Mother's Eyes

"Perhaps by sharing our experiences, we can help you sidestep painful years filled with misdiagnosis and misdirection."

It's like the square-peg-in-the-round-hole, only worse. I'm a triangle. And the only way I'm going to fit into that round hole is to shave off all my edges—or shrink a lot." Joseph Hughes to his mother, on the topic of his school experience.

Maybe you are a parent feeling desperate and alone because your smart kid is "lazy" and "underachieving," and you're looking for help. You may even feel silly reading an article about "giftedness" when your child is not making all As—maybe not even passing!

Though Joseph's standardized scores were clearly in the gifted range, no one particularly commented beyond, "He is a very smart boy." I already knew that, but because he wasn't doing calculus in kindergarten or reading Solschenizyn in second grade, "giftedness," as I understood it, didn't seem relevant. All attention focused on learning differences (aka weaknesses)—no one ever suggested that perhaps the strengths (40-point discrepancy between respectable lowest and very impressive highest scores) might warrant as much or more consideration.

"Things started to go wrong"–almost from the day he started school. Looking back at pictures, I can see it—in his eyes, the strain of his smile.

The school work was literally a no-brainer, but behavior was a constant problem. Wouldn't sit in chair ("ADHD"). Wouldn't do work. Wouldn't wait for instructions ("lack of cooperation"). But it was more than academic. He left pep rallies without permission ("not following rules"), held hands over his ears, crying, distraught (overly sensitive). Wouldn't dress out for PE ("non-compliant;") though subsequently we learned that all the arms going into a bucket tangled with uniforms was simply overwhelming (overexcitable). He fell asleep in class after class (induced by oversensitivity to fluorescent flicker we later learned). He got into fights; no, he got into other people's fights, unable to resist the need to step in and stop a perceived injustice.

Then, as he grew older, he didn't "measure up" academically in the school's viewpoint either. Written work seemed disjointed, almost incoherent—unless someone discussed it with him to discover the huge leaps of logic and reasoning that carried him from place to place. When creating art, the pencil was snatched from his hand to demonstrate how to do it "right." To essay questions, he responded with three-word responses (though if you asked about the subject, he could tell you all about it!). He was the first student to be truly unable to do the freshman bug collection, which required catching and "killing beautiful creatures of life for a grade." Could that be the kind of thing that made classmates think him weird?

Dysgraphia or other LDs? Defiance? Laziness? Or could it be the difficulty of reducing into words—something big, beautiful and complex like Monet's "Waterlilies" seen through the lens of thousands of individual, remarkable strokes and incredible blends of colors? Perhaps it is only evidence of being terribly misunderstood.

About this time, an acquaintance—who subsequently became a dear friend to whom I will be eternally grateful—observed Joseph very briefly and listened to my concerns and frustrations. She had the boldness to speak up, commenting unequivocally that he was gifted. Nonsense! What in this picture looked gifted–at least as I viewed it at the time. She opened for me the door to "gifted land." I began digging and reading. James Webb's *Misdiagnosis* was seminal. I scoured SENG articles, Hoagie's links. Finally, the pieces began to come together in a way that made sense—in a way that fit what I saw and felt and lived. These kids literally see—and feel—the world through different eyes.

I felt enlightened but could not seem to make others accept this alternate side of giftedness. Schools, counselors—they didn't get it, or they didn't buy it. He's bright enough, but mostly he's lazy, unmotivated and non-compliant, they insisted. While my heart told me these were symptoms, not "the disease," I waffled, doubt lurking at the corners of my mind, because I was unable to find human beings in my community who did anything more than nod at me pleasantly as if I were nuts.

Joseph's "serious blow" came at the guidance, insistence even, of well-meaning professionals who assured me they "got" giftedness, but who absolutely did not. And it was going to get even worse, because Joseph did not bend to the expectation, to comply, to be broken in the way a wild horse is broken.

Finally, I found the courage to stand up to conventional wisdom. I set out to turn the experts in "gifted land" into people. We traveled to meet them. We participated in SENG conferences, Joseph and I together. We found an incredibly supportive community. The tragedy is that I didn't find the answer—or even the right questions—before now. And how I looked! I read and searched. Consulted professionals. Yes, I'm probably guilty of having made Joseph feel like a lab rat. I had a need to understand how I could help make life less painful for him. I considered every route on the map—without ever knowing that I was on the wrong map! I can only imagine how many gifted children—and their parents—might be similarly suffering, feeling frighteningly alone, because of misunderstanding about what "giftedness" looks like—even with the guidance of "professionals."

Did he ever really have learning differences? ADHD? I don't know. And I no longer care. Because I choose to embrace Joseph's brilliance. Not intellectual—that's too limiting. I mean that rock-solid (stubborn) inner core that will define success on its own terms, remaining true to self no matter what. I mean teasing out what lies in the gaps. It means covering my eyes to all that seems "normal" and reopening them to all the other paths. It means dwelling in the world of possibilities, celebrating the quirky, frustrating, confusing, beautiful brilliance that shines from this son of mine.

Joseph Hughes's first novel, Armorica, *was released in 2010. Join Joe's international Facebook Fan Club, started by friends at the SENG Teen Program.*

- *Armorica: http://www.ARMORICAworld.com*
- *Fan Club: https://www.facebook.com/groups/10624823451 5/*

Holly Hughes continues to support her son's passions and talents and to advocate for gifted children who are at risk for falling through the cracks of our educational systems.

Why We Homeschooled

By Lisa Rivero

Every gifted homeschooling story starts with an individual child and family. That's how I began a presentation in Hartford, Connecticut, at the New England Conference for the Gifted, co-sponsored by SENG. The topic was "homeschooling as a way to meet social-emotional needs," and preparing the talk gave me an opportunity to think back on our ten years of homeschooling with a perspective that wasn't possible while we were in the middle of it.

Why did we homeschool? The short answer is that it was the best educational and social-emotional fit for our son and family.

Here is the longer answer that I presented in Hartford, my "top ten reasons" that I am glad we homeschooled:

1. Control over the use of labels.

Learning at home allowed us to help our son to understand the differences inherent in giftedness without putting undue focus on being gifted as his primary identity. As a young friend of mine put it recently, giftedness, when overemphasized or praised for its own sake, can easily become something one always must work to defend, what Carol Dweck describes as the "fixed mindset." Children and adults with a fixed mindset have the "single goal of proving themselves—in the classroom, in their careers, and in their relationships. Every situation calls for a confirmation of their intelligence, personality, or character."

2. Individuation of grade levels.

Homeschooling allowed our son to accelerate in individual subjects by self-study, distance learning gifted high school courses, and part-time on-campus university classes, without the need for formal grade acceleration. Just as important, it allowed him to have the "prolongation of opportunities to explore and investigate" on his own, what David Elkind writes is "what intellectually talented youngsters need most."

3. Sleep—enough of it and at optimal times.

Research has linked sleep deficits to underachievement, obesity, and memory and attention problems (Bronson). Parents know how difficult it is for teens to get enough sleep with a full schedule of classes, extracurricular activities, and homework, especially long hours of honors and AP homework. Because of the efficiency of homeschooling, the need to burn the midnight LED light bulb was rare to nonexistent.

4. Time to learn to understand and manage perfectionism.

The flexibility of not assigning grades to learning, especially during our son's younger years, was a tremendous help in his learning to manage what Mary Elaine Jacobsen calls the gifted person's innate "urge to perfect." Barbara Clark, author of the widely used gifted education textbook *Growing Up Gifted*, writes, "under the threat of grades, bright students balk at venturing into the unknown or trying any area in which they are not sure they will succeed." Homeschooling didn't make our son's perfectionism go away, but it did give him time to do most of his learning for the sheer joy of it, so that when he did have to face GPAs and class ranks in college, he was old enough to have some broader perspective on what they do and don't mean.

5. Time for travel and other activities.

During our homeschooling years, we took many trips during off-season travel that would have been difficult to fit into a busy high school schedule, such as visits to Washington, D.C., Philadelphia, New York, Princeton, London, and my family's farm in South Dakota. Our son was also able to have a role in three plays with a local children's theater company, each of which consisted of twenty performances, without having to make up class days or exams.

6. An introvert-tailored education.

Marti Olsen Laney, author of *The Hidden Gifts of the Introverted Child*, writes that some of the traits of introverts are that they "are fatigued by long hours of socializing, even with good friends" and they "need time alone to recharge energy levels." As an adult, I know that I learn and work better when I have a good chunk of my day alone or with one or two people. Why would we expect introverted children to be any different?

7. Lifelong learning and growth.

This advantage is true for both children and parents. Because education is something that happens within the homeschooling family and the broader community, children see firsthand that learning doesn't stop on graduation day. An added bonus for homeschooling parents is that they often reawaken their own passion for learning, revisiting subjects they may have forgotten or even truly learning them for the first time.

8. Mixed-age learning and socialization.

Susan Jackson and Vicky Moyle write that "age-based segregation" is one of the roadblocks to social-emotional growth for gifted children. Our homeschooling literature and writing group included over a dozen students ranging in age from eight to eighteen, allowing learning to happen according to ability level rather than age.

9. Informal social-emotional mentoring.

Mixed-age learning and socializing allowed us to look for and take advantage of opportunities for our son to be mentored by adults and older teens who were comfortable with their giftedness and who lived their intensity with grace and confidence.

10. Quality and quantity family time.

Now that our son is a senior in college, all three of us are grateful for the time we had together in his elementary and high school years, strengthening what Annemarie Roeper calls the "lifeline between parents and child:"

> I would like to impress parents with the reality of the need of the child and that the first requirement is that there be a bond, a lifeline, between parents and child. In my experience, I have found that the solidity of this relationship is the greatest reason that a child will come through the difficult times to which they are often exposed. No matter how isolated some of the very highly gifted feel, they maintain a healthy Self if they feel that their parents

are truly on their side. Many children have told me their parents are their best friends and they could not handle life without them.

Ask the Right Questions

I always feel the need to provide disclaimers when I write or speak about homeschooling:

- *I would never tell any family they should homeschool.*
- *Homeschooling isn't a good fit for every gifted child or every family.*
- *I'm a strong proponent of public education.*
- *I am a huge fan of educators both in and out of the classroom (and I am one myself).*

The question isn't whether anyone *should* homeschool or if homeschooling is a good idea or if it works in general.

For anyone considering homeschooling, the right question is simply this: Is homeschooling a good idea for your child and family?

References

Bronson, P. (2007, Oct. 7). Snooze or lose? *New York Magazine*. Retrieved October 31, 2010, from nymag.com/news/features/38951

Clark, B. (1997). Growing up gifted: Developing the potential of children at home and at school (5th ed.). Upper Saddle River, NJ: Prentice Hall, 440.

Dweck, C. (2007). *Mindset: The new psychology of success.* New York: Ballantine Books, 6.

Elkind, D. (1987). *Miseducation: Preschoolers at risk.* New York: Knopf, 153.

Jackson, S., & Moyle, V. F. (2009). Inner awakening, outward journey: The intense gifted child in adolescence. In S. Daniels & M. M. Piechowski (Eds.), *Living with intensity: Understanding the sensitivity, excitability, and emotional development of gifted children, adolescents, and adults* (pp. 68-69). Scottsdale, AZ: Great Potential Press

Jacobsen, M. E. (2000). The gifted adult: A revolutionary guide for liberating everyday genius. New York: Ballantine Books.

Laney, M. O. (2005). The hidden gifts of the introverted child: Helping your child thrive in an extroverted world. New York: Workman, 14.

Roeper, A. M. (2003). *The emotional needs of the gifted child.* Retrieved October 31, 2010, from www.sengifted.org

---

Lisa Rivero lives in Milwaukee, Wisconsin where she is a writer and Adjunct Associate Professor at Milwaukee School of Engineering. Some of her published books include *Creative Home Schooling* and *The Smart Teens' Guide to Living with Intensity*, and she writes the blog "Creative Synthesis" for *Psychology Today*.

Benny and Me: A Father Sees Himself Through His Son

By Michael Postma

I t was a miserable day in the fall of 2001 when we got our first glimpse of what our lives would be like for the next 20-odd years. We were a young family: a mom, a dad, one young daughter in elementary school, a newborn, and a young lad, Ben.

Ben had always been a very alert boy, one who needed little sleep and had eyes that betrayed a deep longing for information. To say he was curious would be an understatement. As a boy, Ben was constantly getting into everything – taking things apart, exploring, sneaking, finding trouble even where trouble could not possibly be found. On this particular fall day, while mom was occupied with the baby, Ben covered his upper torso with marker before dressing himself, shirt on backwards; head through the arm hole; and, of course, no pants. Armed with a small army of rubber snakes, he decided to find the local park. Dog in tow, he jimmied the lock on the back door and made his way to the park about a quarter of a mile away. One frantic hour later, Ben arrived home via the back seat of a police cruiser, thanks in part to the intervention of a Good Samaritan neighbor who had sensed that something was amiss.

We learned, the hard way sometimes (and with much consternation on my part), that dealing with Ben was going to take a little extra. You see, I work in the field of gifted and talented education and, by 2001, already had some experience working with what we have since labeled the twice- or multi-exceptional child. Ben, it turned out, had Asperger's Syndrome, something that I, the so-called expert, didn't see in my own child. Nor did I see it in myself. Yet, as we grew up together, I saw and relived my own childhood as a multi-exceptional student through living with, chasing, laughing, lecturing, supporting, admonishing, dragging, and, yes, advocating for Ben.

First Experiences With School

As a student in pre-school, Ben refused to play with the other students or engage in whole-class learning, preferring to spend his time exploring and investigating his interest areas.

Flashback: Why doesn't everyone love Geography?...Why won't my fourth grade buddies talk to me about the historical implications of Alexander's conquest of Persia?...I just spent my entire night with a flash light reading about the man...Uh-oh, the teacher is saying something to me...I need to slump down a little farther, perhaps she will see over me...kids are looking at me...shame, panic, anxiety.

Eventually, we pulled him out of pre-school to accommodate his strong desire to remain at home. We discovered that home was his comfort zone and saw that he would struggle (and does so even today) with the transition from that comfort zone to any other place – any place, that is, where he was expected to interact with strangers.

When it was time for kindergarten, I felt that something was amiss as I witnessed a school administrator give Ben a timed, kindergarten readiness exam. Hood pulled over his head, Ben answered some of the educator's questions in a whisper and simply refused to respond to others. "He knows these answers," I screamed in my head. "Why won't he say anything?" Every now and then he peaked out at me with a look of pure fear.

Flashback: Something is knocking at the back of my brain...a memory perhaps...testing, testing, testing...anxiety, blankness...failing.

Ben was formally admitted to this private school, but with some apprehension. All seemed well until later that fall. Much of the work coming home either had large "incomplete" or "unsatisfactory" labels stamped on them or what appeared to be oceans of red ink, while most of his classmates' papers were covered with smiley face stickers and pluses. We waited in trepidation for the first parent/teacher conference. His teacher was concerned. Ben didn't seem to be paying attention; and, while not a behavior problem, he wasn't "up-to-speed." He also refused to speak. Perhaps, I thought to myself at that time, there isn't much interesting within the classroom to speak about; but, having learned some social mannerisms through the years, I refrained. Was there something we were missing? Surely the teacher would let us in on the secret. No, she wanted him to apply himself – no suggestions, no solutions, no accommodations, no changes.

Life in kindergarten did not improve for Ben. His absences were up, learning was down, and intervention was nowhere to be found. As the year came to a close, the school announced its intentions to retain Ben. He just wasn't ready for kindergarten, they said. But he's six, loves art, and is great with numbers, we countered. He's just not ready, they stated. But Ben will be seven and still in kindergarten, we started but slowly trailed off. See you next year, they beamed. Good bye, we muttered. Good riddance, whispered Ben. Bad genes, they thought.

How could this have happened? Kindergarten is supposed to be a fun, positive learning experience for children, the launching pad that jump-starts the rest of your life. Now what? "It's okay, Dad," Benny ventured. "I really don't have to go Shear. I think I already know everything I need to know to survive." I agreed.

What's In A Name?

Our first breakthrough occurred that following summer. In desperation, we spoke with a local public school principal. As we nervously began to tell our tale, expecting the same results, the principal held up her hand. "Have you had Ben tested for Asperger's?" You've got to be kidding me. I have worked with twice-exceptional children before, but my son? Slowly, the plot was unraveling in my mind. How embarrassing it was to have all that education, all that learning, all that practical experience, and not see those traits within my own son.

Flashback: Asperger's...Asperger's...his social anxiety, his clumsiness, his apparent reading disability, his intensity, his sensitivity, his mathematical wizardry, his hood....my social mishaps, my intensity, my fanaticism with social sciences, my apparent Obsessive Compulsive Disorder (ask my wife), my lack of empathy...Ben was me and I was Ben, and yet we we're so different. Asperger's.

It was starting to come together. Eventually, Ben was given an IEP (Individualized Education Program) based on his reading and speech delays. His anxiety was so high that the autism spectrum disorder testing could never be completed. The IEP, however, did mention the high probability of its existence, based on the numerous symptoms he displayed.

Ben began to improve due to the immense and intense efforts and indescribable caring of his teachers. He made a few friends, generally went to school without a lot of resistance, and even learned to love baseball...well, at least the hitting part. While transitions were still difficult, and the Asperger's was still prevalent, at the very least Ben was making progress and had formed a close bond with his teacher (who, incidentally, looped the following year into second grade, much to our delight). It takes a special teacher to enjoy, even welcome, the challenges that Ben brought to the classroom.

Moving Forward

They say (whoever they are) that all good things must come to an end, and so they did. By mid-March of second grade, Ben's teacher left on maternity leave; and I think Ben decided to go on leave as well. Despite the heroic efforts of the new teacher, the principal, and numerous others, Ben spent the majority of his days with the social worker or at home. A week into the new teacher's tenure, Ben began to sob uncontrollably. The intensity of change combined with his penchant for over-excitability completely overwhelmed him. Then we moved.

Flashback: I am sitting at my desk in third grade in anticipation....Phys Ed. was next. I loved sports. It was one thing I excelled at and the kids wanted me on their team. How was I supposed to know that strange kids weren't supposed to be athletic? "Boys and girls, because you were late coming in from recess and talking in the halls, we will not be going outside for Phys Ed. We are going to write about what we learned from this experience." My body is beginning to quiver... I can't think, function...tears, more tears...why am I crying...I'm almost nine.

New house, new city, new school. The first day of school

Ben would not get out of bed. Realizing the transition was going to be rough, I allowed him an extra 15 minutes to sleep. The first day of school is always rough especially after a summer filled with catching snakes, building elaborate habitats, and other stimulating activities. This time there was a new school involved as well.

I went back to check on Ben's progress. Do I pull him out of bed, dress him, carry him to the car, and drag him into school? Or do I use more gentle persuasive tactics? I would recommend the latter, but on this occasion, a little flustered, I chose the former. Within minutes I was chasing Ben through the woods — me in my office clothes, Ben in his underwear and socks.

There were many other days like this before that daily morning ritual began to improve. The remedy? Negotiation and compromise. We worked with Ben's array of teachers and incorporated into his IEP a "break day" every few weeks, a day in which he could stay home, explore, relax, and generally release any pent-up anxiety. These break days also worked as a motivational tactic for getting him to school regularly and on time. He also got little breaks on a daily basis within the school day to have some quiet time or release some anxiety through physical activity in the gymnasium or the motor room, another effective intervention to get him through the daily grind.

The Future Is Unwritten

Ben is now ten years old and attending a school that not only understands but also goes to extreme measures to make accommodations for the twice-exceptional child, truly rare in the era of modern schooling. Although he struggles with the concept of school, he is making progress, as is his Dad. However, I worry — about puberty, middle school, high school, girls, teachers, drugs, alcohol, relationships, and more. Ben is just beginning the journey. I am about half-way through, and all those obstacles plague my outlook and expectations for Ben. Why? I have experienced them all: the embarrassment of puberty; the inability to socialize with the opposite sex in a normal manner or develop deep relationships with people; the dark memory that is middle school; the compensation of alcohol dependency to mask my social dysfunction; the lack of a true, empathetic, and understanding social support network; a spiritual quest for God that emphasizes relationship (one I had to pursue from an intellectual stand-point that continues to this day); and the deep depressions of not fitting in which lasted for years before I sought medical assistance.

Ben doesn't know that I struggled through life just as he is struggling. I struggled despite my constant parachute (one that carried me through even the most difficult of times) – athletics. Unfortunately, Ben has yet to find his own personal parachute. So, I wait and I worry and I protect. I also hope – hope that Ben will find a companion, a friend who understands when my wife and I are no longer around. Ben does know that I haven't always been the greatest father. However, he does understand that I love him dearly and will continue to marvel at his unique thoughts, ideas, and creations, even during moments of challenge and frustration.

Life doesn't ask us what kinds of kids we want. Neither does it send us an advanced checklist of qualities we would like to see in our children. We must deal with the circumstances that we are given, whether we believe it is fair or not. Would I have changed my makeup, or Benny's, given the opportunity? Perhaps, I don't know. However, living with it has forced me to adapt, to persevere, and to develop resiliency skills that continue to assist me to this very day. The field knows much more about students with Autism Spectrum Disorders (ASD) now, than we ever have. I expect that these advances will make life for Benny a little easier to navigate; however, there are no guarantees. So we continue this journey, he and I, and we hope. We hope that tomorrow will bring a kinder, more understanding world – a world that values our abilities and appreciates our shortcomings; a world that accommodates our differences and respects our right to learn at our own pace; a world that laughs with us and not at us; and, perhaps most importantly, a world that allows us to breathe.

For additional information on the Overexcitabilities that can accompany Asperger's Syndrome, see the following:

Dawbrowski, K. (1964). *Positive Disintegration.* Boston: Little Brown & Co.

Mendaglio, S. (2008). *Dawbrowski's Theory of Positive Disintegration.* Scottsdale, AZ: Great Potential Press.

Daniels, S., & Piechowski, M. M. (Eds.). (2009). Living with intensity: Understanding the sensitivity, excitability, and emotional development of gifted children, adolescents, and adults. Scottsdale, AZ: Great Potential Press.

Piechowski, M. M. (2006)."Mellow out" they say. If I only could: Intensities and sensitivities of the young and bright. Madison, WI: Yunasa Books.

Michael Postma is Executive Director at Metrolina Regional Scholars Academy. His education includes degrees in history and education, a Master's degree in gifted and talented education, and an Ed. D in Critical Pedagogy (ABD) from the University of St. Thomas. As the father of two children with Asperger's Syndrome, Michael has a developed a special interest in the realm of the twice-exceptional child.

Dear SENG:

"Gifted Adults" — A Personal Experience

By Helen Prince

Recently, I was surfing on the Internet in search of an article about adult giftedness and came across "Gifted Adults" on the SENG website. As I was reading the article, a surge of normalcy swept over me. What a great sensation it is to feel "normal" when one often feels like an eccentric recluse who can't seem to get where everyone else is at. I believe that knowing one is gifted is as great a gift as the giftedness itself. I wish to share with you my own experience as a gifted adult, how I came to be aware of my own giftedness, and the impact it has had on my life.

I come from a family of nine. My father was illiterate and worked as a labourer. My stay-at-home mom had attained a Grade 6 education. They worked hard and were caring parents with high moral standards. They were a humble people, who were unconcerned with social status. They went about their lives in a simple, unassuming manner, yet did not meet community approval. I concluded that we were average, and that others seemed rather odd in comparison. I'm not sure when the tables turned, but at some point, I found myself believing that others were average, and that it was I who was odd.

195

I dropped out of school after Grade 9, got married, had a son, and worked in a variety of clerical jobs. Ten years later, being consumed by a burning desire for knowledge, I enrolled in a university program. (It did not occur to me to finish high school first.) I completed a Bachelor in Theology (Civil), a Bachelor in Theology (Ecclesiastical), a Bachelor in Education, a Master of Arts (Religious Studies), Foundational Studies in Philosophy, a Specialist in Religious Education, a Certificate in Catholic Education Leadership, and the professional principal's program. I taught at the primary, junior, intermediate, senior, and adult divisions, as well as coordinated Additional Qualification courses for teachers. The majority of my teaching career was in the area of World Religions and Philosophy. I wrote an interactive play about World Religions, and a teacher's manual, student workbook and storybook on how to teach World Religions at the junior level. I sat on committees, coached volleyball, designed showcases, and volunteered to participate in anything innovative in education. A few years ago, I changed career paths, and entered into Adult Basic Literacy which is, without doubt, my true love. At a personal level, I enjoy opera, theatre, philosophy, meditation, quantum physics, computers and the study of human diversity.

I became a teacher first and foremost because my heart ached for my dad, who was not given the opportunity to learn to write his own name; and second, because I am intrigued by all things intellectual. I often wonder if the two reasons are not intimately interconnected. While I love teaching, I am somewhat disappointed in the lack of intellect that I have found in the field of education. Furthermore, despite my qualifications and absolute passion for the study of religions, I was not successful in attaining a department head position; and, despite being a qualified principal, I was never considered for even a vice-principal job. While there may be many reasons for this, I find myself not at the top of the likable list other than with family, close friends, and Mensans. My heightened sensitivity to air quality, light, noise and other stimulation makes me appear fussy and self-centered. I try my best to say as little as possible, but there are situations where I am so overwhelmed that I sometimes slip up and ask for a window to be opened or the sound to be turned down. There is doubtless a bit of panic in my voice, and the request seems excessive to many, and I suffer a sense of shame for not being able to assimilate. As well, I have an overactive sense of duty and morality. I am demanding on myself and others, and am absolutely unwilling to do anything that I feel is morally questionable. My solid moral stance can be quite inopportune because, in the end, my conscience must rule even over my supervisor's preferences, and that is not a favourable position to find oneself.

At the age of 57 and despite four university degrees and a very active and happy career, albeit without promotion, I had convinced myself of my own mediocrity, and even wondered if I might be a little less than average. As a teacher, I thought a better understanding of my own psycho-educational profile could assist me in better serving my adult students, many of whom have similar backgrounds to me. I completed the Wechsler Adult Intelligence Scale and was astounded when it revealed an I.Q. score that placed me in the top 2 percent of the population. Even after the psychologist informed me of this, it took me one year to join Mensa because I was afraid that there was some sort of error and I would soon be found out.

My discovery of giftedness left me to wonder why I was not previously informed. I was a cooperative and respectful student, who learned new concepts easily, worked very hard and was a high achiever. Yet not once can I recall being told that I was even adequate, let alone gifted. As a teacher today, I look back at my childhood and reflect that perhaps poverty is one of the reasons that giftedness might be overlooked. I think that even with today's heightened social awareness, we continue to favour the children of the affluent for academic programs, and suppose that only the doctor's or professor's children can be gifted. I believe there is a deep-rooted error in a still classist society that robs many gifted children of the awareness of their giftedness; and so we are doomed to enter adulthood, as probably did our parents, believing in our own mediocrity. I know this occurs not only because it happened to me, but because in the three years that I have been teaching adult basic literacy, I have identified three students I believe to be gifted. With a grade nine education, they read and write at a university level. Their thinking contains that profound insight associated with giftedness. There is a sparkle in their eyes that cannot be mistaken. There is confusion in their lives because they are not aware that they are gifted. What a great loss of human potential that could well have achieved great things for the betterment of our world. Yet, there they are, wondering why they can't achieve a high school diploma and why they feel so odd. What a pity!

Since discovering my own giftedness, life is so much more comprehensible and pleasurable. I get it, now; I am the odd one out. I try so much more to adjust myself accordingly, thus not offending the majority. I go about my work compassionately and seek out creative ventures that will benefit others and my own creative cravings. I do my work quietly and without fanfare so others will not take notice. I socialize more with others like myself so I can have a sense of normalcy as often as possible. I make certain that I take time to play within the boundless boundaries of my own mind. I have come to really like who I am, and to be very thankful to my parents who gave this gift of giftedness to me. Despite the hassles that come with the territory, I wouldn't give up my giftedness for all the kingdoms in the world. The gifted adult need not merely survive, but can flourish so long as one is aware of one's own giftedness and celebrates it in one's own unique way.

Connect with **SENG** Online

Web: http://www.sengifted.org
Facebook: http://www.facebook.com/SENGifted
Twitter: http://www.twitter.com/SENG_gifted

Made in the USA
San Bernardino, CA
07 March 2015